Strength
FOR THE JOURNEY

A 60 Day Devotional for Wisdom & Spiritual Growth

DAVID M. LOCKHART

Copyright © 2022 by David M. Lockhart
All rights reserved. This book or any portion thereof may not be reproduced or used in any manner whatsoever without the express written permission of the publisher except for the use of brief quotations in a book review.

Limits of Liability and Disclaimer of Warranty
The author and publisher shall not be liable for your misuse of this material. This book is strictly for informational purposes. The purpose of this book is to educate and entertain. The author and publisher do not guarantee anyone following these techniques, suggestions, tips, ideas, or strategies will become successful. The author and publisher shall have neither liability nor responsibility to anyone with respect to any loss or damage caused, or alleged to be caused, directly or indirectly by the information contained in this book. Views expressed in this publication do not necessarily reflect the views of the publisher.

Cover: By Triv designsbytriv@gmail.com

Printed in the United States of America
Keen Vision Publishing, LLC
www.publishwithKVP.com
ISBN: 978-1-955316-76-7

To my father, the late Maxie Allen Lockhart, and my mother, Secemonia Miller Lockhart. Thank you for teaching me to treat everyone with dignity and respect. I could not have become the man I am today without my parents, who, through their life, showed and taught me never to give up and how to bounce back from adversity.

TOPIC INDEX

FOREWORD	9
INTRODUCTION	11
TOGETHERNESS IS THE HIGHWAY TO SUCCESS	15
IN GOD'S STRENGTH	19
READY? SET? TAKE A LEAP OF FAITH!	23
GOD HAS A PURPOSE FOR YOUR LIFE	27
STAYING CALM IN A CRISIS	31
STRENGTH TO PUSH THROUGH	35
LET GO AND MOVE FORWARD	39
HOLD TO GOD'S UNCHANGING HAND	43
ON EAGLES' WINGS	47
EMERGENCY BEEPER	51
OVERCOMING THE UNKNOWN	55
BOUNCING BACK FROM ADVERSITY	59
IT'S NOT ALL ABOUT YOU	63
GREENER GRASS	67
DIGGING IN	71

STRENGTH FOR THE JOURNEY

NEVER SEEK REVENGE	**75**
GET OUT OF YOUR COMFORT ZONE	79
A FATHER'S LOVE	**83**
GOD IS WATCHING OVER YOU	87
INCOMING! INCOMING!	**91**
LOOKING ON THE POSITIVE SIDE	95
ALL IN!	**99**
SPIRITUAL IMMATURITY	103
GOD IS YOUR FRONT-WHEEL DRIVE	**107**
MAKING A COMEBACK	111

A FRIEND THAT STICKS

CLOSER THAN A BROTHER	**115**
DON'T BE SCARED!	119
LESSON IN HUMILITY	**123**
RESTORING HOPE TO BROKEN DREAMS	127
THIS CHAPTER IS OVER	**131**
TRUST GOD WHEN YOU CAN'T TRACE HIM	135
YOU CAN'T PLEASE EVERYBODY	**139**
WHAT IS YOUR VISION?	143
DON'T TAP OUT	**147**

IT'S LIKE A JUNGLE

SOMETIMES IT MAKES ME WONDER	151
WALK BY FAITH	**155**
AN UNSHAKEABLE FAITH	159
PRESSURE BURSTS A PIPE	**163**
THIS IS NOT THE FINAL DESTINATION	167
GETTING THROUGH THE TURBULENCE	171

TOPIC INDEX

WHAT IS IN YOUR RUCKSACK?	175
SITUATIONAL AWARENESS	179
END OF THE YEAR INVENTORY	**183**
THE GOD OF A SECOND CHANCE	187
COMBATTING SUICIDAL IDEATION	**191**
HOW HIGH DO YOU ASPIRE TO GO?	195
WORDS MATTER	**199**
ARE YOU PREPARED TO WIN?	203
BE THANKFUL	207
FREEDOM IS NEVER FREE	211
NEVER GIVE UP ON YOUR DREAMS	215
MORE BLESSED TO GIVE THAN RECEIVE	**219**
STAYING ON COURSE	223
HAVING A SERVANT'S HEART	**227**
HIS ROD AND STAFF COMFORT ME	231
DON'T SWEAT THE SMALL STUFF	**235**
DO GOOD TOWARD ALL	239
ENCOURAGING ONE ANOTHER	**243**
GOD WILL PROVIDE	247
OVERCOMING ADVERSITY	**251**
ABOUT THE AUTHOR	255
ACKNOWLEDGMENTS	**256**
CONNECT WITH THE AUTHOR	257

FOREWORD

Did your mother ever tell you not to 'judge a book by it's cover'? Mine did, and I ignored her. I made a mistake, and you are about to benefit from my error in judgement. I met Chaplain David Lockhart at Fort Stewart, Georgia in 1995. He was a brand-new Army chaplain assigned to an infantry battalion next door to my unit. David was quiet, self-effacing, and humble. I walked away from our first meeting convinced that this nice, articulate, well mannered Presbyterian preacher was too 'meek and mild' for the rough, tough infantry soldiers of his new flock.

I was dead wrong. Chaplain Lockhart turned out to be just what the soldiers of 3-15th Infantry Battalion needed. He was a tremendous listener, an empathetic counselor, a great preacher, and an outstanding Army officer. In short, the soldiers loved him and responded to his ministry. He ran with his men, rucked marched with them, went to the field with them and cared for their souls. The man from Harvest, Alabama turned out to be a man of God gifted for God's call to Army chaplaincy and 'tougher than woodpecker lips.'

I have had the wonderful privilege of being a friend of David's ever since our meeting at Fort Stewart. I've watched his career blossom. I've seen his impact at every level of the Army. From tactical units to strategic assignments, from stateside to combat in Iraq, I've seen him minister to soldiers, master the challenges of his assignments and lead men and women to God.

You are about to receive a blessing. The book that follows will inform your mind, inspire your soul, and challenge your heart. David's gift for communication will be evident as he delivers Christian principles and Christ's teachings in pithy, insightful devotions for your daily edification.

I pray you will learn from my mistake and heed my caution; "Don't underestimate what God can do for you through the man from Harvest, Alabama!"

Chaplain (Colonel-Retired)
John Morris

INTRODUCTION

I started writing devotionals at Memphis Theological Seminary in 1992 but I only shared them with the late Dr. Tessie Rae Simmons. Tessie said, "One day, you should write a devotional book. Your devotionals will inspire, encourage and give people hope during difficult times." As the years passed and I began to write devotionals for the Pentagram, an "Independent Newspaper," for the Army based out of Joint Base Myers-Henderson Hall Washington DC, and other Military Bases Newspapers throughout my career. The men and women I served with in the Military encouraged me to write a devotional book for publication.

It was during the summer of 2020 that I finally decided to put my devotionals into a book. Some of the stories are from personal experience, some I read in books, and others were passed down through oral tradition from ministers in the past. In this book, I provide knowledge to some and perhaps, impart knowledge to others. Nevertheless, I hope these devotionals are a blessing to everyone who reads them. I hope you find yourself in several pages of this book and that it leaves you with a passion to share wisdom with others.

Knowledge without actions is like a well-written book left unopened on a shelf; it doesn't benefit anyone. After you read each devotional, ask yourself the following questions:

- How did today's devotional help me to grow spiritually?
- How can I share the wisdom I've gained with family, friends, or strangers who need strength along their journey?

You see, we are all sojourning through life. We need strength day by day to make it on this this journey. This journey called life comes with loneliness, depression, guilt, shame, abandonment, grief, prejudice, heartache, and pain. Especially at the time this book was released, the pandemic has caused many individuals to be stressed and has robbed them of their joy and peace of mind. If we are not careful, life's difficulties can zap our strength and ruin our lives.

Since every location along our journey is new, we often find ourselves wading through unchartered

INTRODUCTION

waters. It is easy to become fearful and worry about the unknowns. However, if we resolve to trust God, no matter how heavy our burdens or how long our nights, He will give us *strength to overcome any obstacles you are facing.* As the Hawkins Family says in the song, "I'm a Pilgrim":

Lord I'm a pilgrim
travelin through
this ole barren land
I want you to please
guide my footsteps
and please hold my hand

Keep pressing, my friend. What is coming is greater than what has been. As you journey to your next destination, allow *Strength for the Journey* to challenge you to grow deeper in God and trust Him for everything you need.

DAY ONE

TOGETHERNESS IS THE HIGHWAY TO SUCCESS

"Go to the ant, you sluggard! Consider her ways and be wise, Which, having no captain, overseer or ruler, Provides her supplies in the summer, And gathers her food in the harvest."
Proverbs 6: 6-8 (NKJV)

The Coronavirus came in abruptly and turned our world upside down. Not only did it turn our world upside down, but it left us all attempting to adapt to what experts are calling our "new normal." It may be hard for some of us to embrace this new normal, especially when they are still trying to develop a strategy to combat it. Coronavirus has changed the way we approach life. Everything was going well, and suddenly, businesses, schools, and entertainment were all shut down. How do we bounce back from chaos? How do we get through this? We can't get through this alone. Do not be a lone ranger and try to get through this without the support of others. We need to lean on each other. As a team, we can get through this together. We can take a page from the ants that "togetherness is the highway that leads to success."

One day, I was observing an anthill. I am sure we all have seen these incredible anthills. It is impressive to watch the ants build their castle and see how each ant contributes. The colonies were prospering and enjoying the work of their labor when suddenly, someone came along and tore the ant's castle apart. Those ants didn't just walk away from the hill; they regrouped and rebuilt the anthill together.

The Bible says in Proverbs 6:6 (NKJV), *"Go to the ant, you sluggard! Consider her ways and be wise."* Ants work as a team, and they understand togetherness. While observing those small ants, what I saw next was amazing. The ants were working very hard, moving fast and swiftly to put the anthill back up. I was surprised by how they helped and supported each other. They got on different ends of the item they were dragging to rebuild the anthills. They also protected each other from harm as they kept other little critters from coming near the hill. As we struggle with what to do next amid this pandemic, we have to take a page from the ants. Let us bounce back from this as a team because "None of us is as smart as all of us. Work together; achieve more." Working together can ameliorate many problems we may be dealing with alone because of Coronavirus.

DAY ONE

APPLICATION

Answer these questions in a journal or notebook to reflect on today's devotional.

1. What can you learn from the ants?
2. What team event can you do virtually this week to alleviate stress and re-energize your team?

> *"I think everybody should study ants. They have an amazing four-part philosophy. Never give up, look ahead, stay positive and do all you can."*
> **Jim Rohn**

STRENGTH FOR THE JOURNEY

Notes & Takeaways

In the space below, write your top three take-aways from this chapter.

DAY TWO

IN GOD'S STRENGTH

"I can do all things through Christ who strengthens me."
Philippians 4:13 (NKJV)

In this passage, Paul concluded that his strength came from God. No matter what came his way, he could endure it because God was there to help him. Paul was actually saying, "I am not trying to endure hardships and tragedies in my own strength."

There are some things in life that you can't handle alone. Some things in life will make you want to give up and quit. However, when you stretch out on God, He gives you that extra boost you need to cross the finish line.

The songwriter who said, "I am leaning and depending on the everlasting arm of God," was correct. Too often, we depend on people to get us through difficult times. There's nothing wrong with having prayer partners, but sometimes their strength is just not enough to comfort you and protect you when you are down and out. If you walk in God's strength, He will provide for you when you can't provide for yourself.

I am reminded of a story about my late cousin, Maxie Wayne, whom we used to call Poochie. He was about sixteen when I was thirteen, and he showed me the correct way to lift weights. I said, "Poochie, there is no way I can lift all those weights." He wanted me to do ten reps. He said, "Don't worry about anything. I got you." I began to lift as he spotted me. I completed the ten reps and got very excited. Jumping up, I said, "Did you see how easily I lifted those heavy weights? I am the man!" He said, "David, before you tell anyone else about the ten reps, you only did three. The other seven were in my strength." I responded, "So, in other words, if you had not helped me, I would not have achieved the ten reps?" He said, "That is correct."

That is what Paul is saying here. When you get weak, God is strong and can make a difference. After all, He will help you get through tough times because His strength is made perfect in our weakness. God is your spotter, and He knows just how much you can bear.

DAY TWO

APPLICATION

Answer these questions in a journal or notebook to reflect on today's devotional.

1. Can you trace times in your life when God was your spotter?
2. How do you apply Philippians 4:13 in your own life?

"Relying on God has to begin all over every day, as if nothing has yet been done."
C.S. Lewis

STRENGTH FOR THE JOURNEY

Notes & Takeaways

In the space below, write your top three take-aways from this chapter.

DAY THREE

READY? SET? TAKE A LEAP OF FAITH!

"God is our refuge and strength, a very present help in trouble."
Psalm 46:1 (NKJV)

I remember 1993, when my nephew Adrian was four years old, and we were at the church that I pastored. My Church Elder put Adrian on the hood of his truck and told him to jump, but Adrian would not jump. He tried to lure Adrian with candy, but he still would not jump. He then asked Adrian if he was scared; Adrian said, "Yes, I am scared." I said to my Elder, "Adrian will jump for me." I stepped in and called out: "Adrian, get ready, get set, and jump!" Adrian took a gigantic leap of faith. My Elder looked in disbelief. He asked Adrian why he jumped for his uncle and not for him. Adrian looked on, smiled, and said, "I trust my uncle because he would never let me fall." Adrian trusted me because he had jumped for me several times in the past, and I never let him fall.

Now let's take a stroll down memory lane. Look back over your life and think about all those times life was very difficult, and you could not see your way clearly. Did God let you fall?

During this crisis, I understand the fear of uncertainty in not knowing when this pandemic will end. Will my family and I get through it? You can rest assured that if you take a leap of faith in the arms of God, you will not fall. If you take a leap of faith, you will stay encouraged even when facing discouraging situations.

The Bible says in Psalm 46:1 (NKJV), *"God is our refuge and strength, a very present help in trouble."* God is with you in the midst of your storm, but you have to put your trust in Him. Remember, through it all, God will be your shelter and protection. Get ready, get set, and take a leap of faith! He is waiting for you to jump. Will you take a leap of faith and trust that God will not let you fall?

DAY THREE

APPLICATION

This week, take a leap of faith and trust God to handle all your problems. Learn how to lean and depend on God to overcome your fears.

> *"Preparation can only take you so far, after that you've got to take a few leaps of faith."*
> **Michael Scofield**

STRENGTH FOR THE JOURNEY

Notes & Takeaways

In the space below, write your top three take-aways from this chapter.

DAY FOUR

GOD HAS A PURPOSE FOR YOUR LIFE

"And we know that all things work together for good to those who love God, to those who are the called according to His purpose."

Romans 8:28 (NKJV)

God has a purpose and plan for your life. However, sometimes we get frustrated because we can't see the results instantly. We are so impatient and don't want to wait on God for anything. We want God to microwave it for us because we don't feel like God is moving swiftly enough. He is taking too long to work out our situations. We feel like we could do it better than God, saying things like, "If I were God, I would have taken care of my problems this way, and everything would be fine right now." I am reminded of a story I heard growing up in North Alabama. The story was about a man standing around a watermelon patch. He backed up against this big oak tree, looked up, and saw these small acorns on this big oak tree. He looked over and saw these big watermelons on those small little vines. He said, "Oh my God, look at what God has done. God has messed up nature. Now, if I were God, I would have put these little acorns on these small watermelon vines, and I would have put these big watermelons on this big oak tree." Around that time, the wind started blowing, and one of the acorns fell from the tree and hit the man on top of the head. He said, "I thank God it was not a watermelon."

See, God knows what He is doing. Just as there was a purpose for the acorn and watermelon, God has a purpose for your life. God knows what is best for you. You may encounter some rough and rocky situations. The valley may get low, and the mountain may get hard to climb, but never forget God has a purpose for our lives. Romans 8:28 (NKJV) says, *"And we know that all things work together for good to those who love God, to those who are the called according to His purpose."* God's plan is to get us to our purposed place. If our lives do not reflect what the scriptures proclaim, it is a layover and not the final destination.

APPLICATION

Answer these questions in a journal or notebook to reflect on today's devotional.

1. What does it mean for you to be called according to His purpose?
2. How do you trust God when you can't see the purpose?

"God's timing is always perfect. Trust His delays. He's got you."

Tony Evans

STRENGTH FOR THE JOURNEY

Notes & Takeaways

In the space below, write your top three take-aways from this chapter.

DAY FIVE

STAYING CALM IN A CRISIS

"'Fear not, for I am with you; Be not dismayed, for I am your God. I will strengthen you, Yes, I will help you, I will uphold you with My righteous right hand.'"

Isaiah 41:10 (NKJV)

When crisis comes, what's our first reaction as human beings? Is it fear? Fear is defined as an emotion induced by a perception of danger or threat. Fear will eventually cause behavioral changes if left untreated, making you act out of character. It will cause you to focus on yourself and forget about the rest of humankind.

This brings me to a topic that has become all too familiar worldwide: Coronavirus SARS-CoV-2, which was identified in late 2019. When the NBA Commissioner shut down NBA games, March Madness was canceled, the Masters Golf Tournament was postponed, and we heard warning after warning to stay away from large crowds, causing people to panic. People were stampeding over each other to buy supplies for themselves, buying an enormous supply of toilet paper, hand sanitizer, and bottled water, not mindful of others needing the same supplies.

I agree we should be proactive in developing a strategy for our families. We should maintain situational awareness, always assessing and mitigating risks. However, remember to stay calm during the crisis, and we will get through it with a peaceful mindset. Amid a crisis, stop, exhale and know that God is in control.

God's Word declares in Isaiah 41:10 that we shouldn't fear or become dismayed or distressed, for the Lord our God will strengthen us. God will encourage us in our times of despair, strengthen us in our times of weakness, guide us in our times of danger, and assure us in our times of anxiety. Together, we will get through this. In times of crisis, we should encourage and support each other.

DAY FIVE

APPLICATION

Answer these questions in a journal or notebook to reflect on today's devotional.

1. Does Isaiah 41:10 speak to your current situation? If so, how?
2. What is your strategy to overcome fear?

> "America was not built on fear. America was built on courage, on imagination and an unbeatable determination to do the job at hand."
>
> **Harry S. Truman**

STRENGTH FOR THE JOURNEY

Notes & Takeaways

In the space below, write your top three take-aways from this chapter.

DAY SIX

STRENGTH TO PUSH THROUGH

"We are pressed on every side, but we still have room to move. We are often in much trouble, but we never give up. People make it hard for us, but we are not left alone. We are knocked down, but we are not destroyed."
2 Corinthians 4:8-9 (NLV)

Lawrence Julius Taylor, Hall of Famer and former American Football Player, played his entire professional career as a linebacker for the New York Giants in the National Football League. Considered one of the greatest players in football history, he has been ranked as the greatest defensive player in NFL history by former players, coaches, media members, and news outlets such as the NFL Network and Sporting News. An ESPN piece on L.T. shows how he had separated his shoulder during an important playoff game. They show him on the sideline, and the pain is so unbearable and severe that he is literally shaking. Guess what he does. He still puts his helmet back on and gets back into the game. The football experts say he took over the game and willed the Giants to victory.

After the game was over, they interviewed L.T. and asked, "How did you, in such pain, will your team to victory?" L.T. said, "Listen, there comes a point in your life where pain, if you play through it, turns into power. When it turns into power, you can't lose."

There will come a point in each of our lives where we have to push through the pain until it turns into power. Life situations will appear to get the best of us; burdens may be heavier than we can imagine ourselves carrying. Nights may be sleepless, and our jobs may be challenging. In those times, we have to remember we're never alone. God promises never to leave nor forsake us. He will strengthen us to push through the pain.

APPLICATION

Answer these questions in a journal or notebook to reflect on today's devotional.

1. How do you seek out ways to push through your pain?
2. What does II Corinthians 4:8-9 mean to you?

"Pain is temporary. It may last a minute, or an hour, or a day, or a year, but eventually, it will subside, and something else will take its place. If I quit, however, it lasts forever."

Lawrence Armstrong

STRENGTH FOR THE JOURNEY

Notes & Takeaways

In the space below, write your top three take-aways from this chapter.

DAY SEVEN

LET GO AND MOVE FORWARD

"Brethren, I do not count myself to have apprehended; but one thing I do, forgetting those things which are behind and reaching forward to those things which are ahead."

Philippians 3:13 (NKJV)

This week, I heard a story about two cousins, Gus and H. L. They went to a Fourth of July party. The party got really good because they made a few too many trips to the punch bowl. The punch bowl had some tasty stuff mixed with the fruit punch. They kept going back to the punch bowl and getting full of the tasty spirits, forgetting the party was located across a lake they would have to row their boat across to get home. When the party was over around four in the morning, they got back in their boat and began rowing it to the other side of the lake to get home. At 5:00 a.m., they were still rowing. At 6:00 a.m., they were still rowing. At 7:00 a.m., the sun came up, and they discovered they had not pulled up the anchor. As a consequence, they kept going where they had already been. Why? They forgot to let go of something that was keeping them from getting to where they were trying to go.

If you are not careful, some stuff you refuse to let go of won't let go of you either. Before you know it, life will become one big merry-go-round; you'll keep going where you've already been and doing what you've already done.

Some of us need to pull up the anchor and let go of the past. Some things are not easy to let go of, but if you don't pull up the anchor and let go, you'll make life miserable for yourself and perhaps others around you. Failure to do so will only rob you of joy, peace of mind, and fulfillment. If you're challenged with letting go, ask God to give you the strength to let go and move forward.

APPLICATION

Make a list of the things you are struggling to let go of, those that need to be forever buried in the eternal tomb of yesterday.

> *"When people walk away from you, let them go. Your destiny is never tied to anyone who leaves you, and it doesn't mean they are bad people. It just means that their part in your story is over."*
>
> **T.D. Jakes**

STRENGTH FOR THE JOURNEY

Notes & Takeaways

In the space below, write your top three take-aways from this chapter.

DAY EIGHT

HOLD TO GOD'S UNCHANGING HANDS

"I made you and I will care for you. I will carry you along and be your Savior."

Isaiah 46:4 (TLB)

I heard a story about a physically challenged boy who entered the Youth Olympic Games to run a one-mile jog around the track. It was a challenge for the young man whose braces made his legs heavy, and his handicap slowed his pace. As he ran half of a mile the way, he could not seem to put one foot in front of the other. He did not have the strength or energy and almost fell. His father recognized that he would lose faith, hope, courage, and determination if he fell or did not finish the race. So the father ran onto the track and held his son's hand.

Holding his father's hand, the boy pushed himself to make every step until he crossed the finish line. The boy was excited; he looked up at his father and said, "Can I go again?" The father said, "I thought you were tired." The boy said, "I may be tired, but I can do it as long as you hold my hand!" Right now, there may be a plethora of problems going on in your life. Some of them may have proliferated out of your control. However, I can promise you that you will get to the finish line if you hold on to God's unchanging hands. God promises to "never leave you or forsake you" (Deuteronomy 31: 6), and he will hold your hands to the finish line.

Isaiah 46:4 explains that while the people believed God for their liberation, they were fatigued and tired from their long wait. This text encouraged them to remember that God would keep them from being overcome by weariness. He would keep His promise; it seemed like a slow pace, but He would move at His time and place. When we hold to God's unchanging hands, our burdens don't seem to be so heavy, circumstances don't seem to be so bad, and problems don't seem to be so difficult. The songwriter said that "God is an on time God, He may not come when you want Him but He is always on time."

DAY EIGHT

APPLICATION

On this journey called life, we will never become a winner or be victorious if we quit. This week, learn to hold on to God's unchanging hands because quitting is not an option.

> *"I have held many things in my hands, and I have lost them all; but whatever I have placed in God's hands, that I still possess."*
>
> **Martin Luther**

STRENGTH FOR THE JOURNEY

Notes & Takeaways

In the space below, write your top three take-aways from this chapter.

DAY NINE

ON EAGLES' WINGS

"But those who wait on the LORD Shall renew their strength; They shall mount up with wings like eagles, They shall run and not be weary, They shall walk and not faint."
Isaiah 40:31 (NKJV)

The eagle has muscle power. Her bones and flesh were designed by the Creator so that she could fly directly into a storm. While other animals take cover when a storm is coming, the eagle can perceive a storm coming days earlier, fly directly into it, do a kind of 180-degree turn, and move with it. When the storm speeds up, the eagle speeds up; when the storm slows down, the eagle slows down. After a while, you will see the eagle rise above that storm unharmed and unhurt. That is what God is saying to those of us who wait upon Him. He will give us the strength to rise above the storms in our lives.

When teaching her eaglets how to fly, the eagle puts them on the pinions of her wings, takes them high up, and drops them off the pinions. She does this several times until they catch on and learn how to fly independently. During the process, it seems like they will fall to the ground while going through basic training, but right before they fall, the mother eagle swoops down and puts them on the pinions of her wings. God does the same for us. When it seems like we will fall and not make it through, He swoops down, picks us up, and carries us through our most difficult times, just like an eagle. On eagles' wings, God's grace is sufficient. On eagles' wings, God's mercy is everlasting, and His love is abundant.

The lyrics of "On Eagle's Wings" summarize this devotion. They say, "You who dwell in the shelter of the Lord, who abides in His shadow for life: Say to the Lord, 'My refuge, my rock in whom I trust!' And He will raise you up on eagles' wings, bear you on the breath of dawn, make you to shine like the sun."

DAY NINE

APPLICATION

Answer these questions in a journal or notebook to reflect on today's devotional.

1. How does it encourage you to know that God will give you the strength to rise above the storms in your life?
2. Make a list of the things you need to rise above this week.

> *"The eagle has no fear of adversity. We need to be like the eagle and have a fearless spirit of a conqueror!"*
>
> **Joyce Meyer**

STRENGTH FOR THE JOURNEY

Notes & Takeaways

In the space below, write your top three take-aways from this chapter.

DAY TEN

EMERGENCY BEEPER

"'Call to Me, and I will answer you, and show you great and mighty things, which you do not know.'"

Jeremiah 33:3 (NKJV)

A few years ago, I heard a story about a man named Robert from Utah who was skiing, enjoying life, and riding gracefully through the trees. Without warning, the snow raced, and the ground collapsed. He was swept away, flying through the air in a large avalanche, which caught him from behind. The avalanche overtook him, and around him was nothing but white. He was buried alive, seven feet deep under the snow. Robert testified that, in a real sense, he was ready to give up. He had no hope of surviving the avalanche. He concluded that his life was over; an avalanche of snow had him buried too deep for him to reach the surface of the snow. You may have never been on a mountain slope, but you know about the avalanches of adversity that come in life.

They come without warning; they come in pairs. If it's not one thing, it's another. When you put a fire out in one place, a fire pops up in another. Do you remember those avalanches of adversity in your life that robbed you of your faith in God?

Robert was buried in snow and ready to give up, but all of a sudden, he heard some voices above him. The voices said, "We are here. We picked up the signal on your emergency beeper," because skiers wear an emergency beeper that goes off whenever an avalanche comes so the rescue team can find them. They said, "We picked up your signal. We are digging right now. Hold on because we are right here. Don't give up because we are here." Suddenly, he developed energy and strength that he did not have before. Why? He heard a voice from above, and that voice gave him some energy. He was able to hold on, but he had to wait.

Somebody needs to know today that God has picked up your signal. Just hold on and have faith. Don't give up because help is on the way. No matter how difficult your situation may be, keep your "emergency beeper" (prayer, faith, and hope) on because God will pick up your signal.

DAY TEN

APPLICATION

Answer these questions in a journal or notebook to reflect on today's devotional.

1. How can you keep your emergency beeper on through prayer, faith, and hope?
2. What does Jeremiah 33:3 mean to you?

> *"There is a tomorrow after a disaster, and it's sometimes hard to remember that in the midst of it."*
>
> **Sheri Fink**

STRENGTH FOR THE JOURNEY

Notes & Takeaways

In the space below, write your top three take-aways from this chapter.

DAY ELEVEN

OVERCOMING THE UNKNOWN

"The LORD is my light and my salvation; Whom shall I fear? The LORD is the strength of my life; Of whom shall I be afraid?"
Psalms 27:1 (NKJV)

In April 2007, I found out I had lung cancer. The doctor said, "We need to do surgery right away," but I could not give him an answer right away because this was unknown territory to me. A week later, I asked for a second opinion, and it was confirmed. I went through the pity party for a few days: "Lord, why me? I did everything you asked me to do. I always went above and beyond in taking care of soldiers, family members, and DOD civilians."

So finally I agreed to have the surgery. The doctor said, "I can't promise you how it will come out, but I will do the best I can." I went home that night, and my mind began to race with the unknowns. Many unknown variables shook my faith, and there were so many questions I had to deal with: "Is this the end of my journey on earth? Has it spread beyond my lungs? How many chemo or radiation treatments will I have to go through? Will I bounce back to my old self? Will I be able to physically endure deployment? Will I be able to continue in the military?" I was worried because I had never had to deal with so many unknowns at this level.

I prayed and read different scriptures from the Bible to encourage myself, and I will never forget what happened around the fifth day. That night, Psalm 27:1, which I had not been reading, was heavy on my mind and in my heart: "The LORD is my light and my salvation; Whom shall I fear? The LORD is the strength of my life; Of whom shall I be afraid?" Psalm 27:1 (NKJV) Instantly, the fear went away, and faith took over. I realized that there was no need to fear or worry because God was in control. The surgery was successful, and later on, in my career, I deployed to Iraq and Afghanistan.

I understand we are in unchartered water with this Coronavirus. You may be fearful and worrying about the unknown. There are a lot of unknown variables. However, I can assure you that if you trust God, He will give you the strength to overcome the unknown, no matter how heavy your burdens or how long your nights.

DAY ELEVEN

APPLICATION

This week, let's try to put the unknown in God's hands and stop worrying because worrying has never paid one bill. Worrying has never eased anyone's pain, solved one problem, or made any heavy load lighter. There is no need to worry because God will give you the strength to overcome the unknown.

> *"We all have a fear of the unknown what one does with that fear will make all the difference in the world."*
> **Lillian Russell**

STRENGTH FOR THE JOURNEY

Notes & Takeaways

In the space below, write your top three take-aways from this chapter.

DAY TWELVE

BOUNCING BACK FROM ADVERSITY

"We are pressed on every side, but we still have room to move. We are often in much trouble, but we never give up. People make it hard for us, but we are not left alone. We are knocked down, but we are not destroyed."

2 Corinthians 4:8-9 (NLV)

John Madden, former football coach and television commentator, coined the phrase YAC, which means yards after contact. He noticed that great running backs like Jim Brown, Walter Payton, and Emmitt Smith gained more yards after being hit by the opposing players. No matter how hard an individual player or group of players hit them, they would keep going forward. These great running backs kept making yards after the contact. The more Brown, Payton, and Smith were hit, the more they wanted the ball. They always bounced back from adversity because they never gave up on a play.

Sometimes life becomes challenging, and we feel like giving up on the play. We don't want to come out of the huddle and compete anymore. Instead, we look toward the sidelines for a replacement. However, Paul encourages us to bounce back from adversity. We can't escape from all of our troubles, but where is our YAC to get us through them? We can't throw in the towel, so where is our YAC? Even though people sometimes make life hard for us, where is our YAC? Paul says that yes, people make it hard for us, but God is in the midst of the adversity we are going through. We have to keep going forward when we get knocked down because we have not been destroyed.

Brothers and sisters, it may seem like we are constantly facing adversity. Things around us seem to be at their worst. Even when people lie to us and talk behind our backs, and we have to endure hateful and hurtful words, we will get through it. We will get through our adversities because our YAC is stronger than what is trying to stop us.

DAY TWELVE

APPLICATION

Answer these questions in a journal or notebook to reflect on today's devotional.

1. What will help you to remember and hold on to God's guaranteed and sure hope of deliverance?
2. How has trusting in God helped you bounce back from adversity?

> *"Sometimes adversity is what you need to face in order to become successful."*
>
> **Zig Ziglar**

STRENGTH FOR THE JOURNEY

Notes & Takeaways

In the space below, write your top three take-aways from this chapter.

DAY THIRTEEN

IT'S NOT ALL ABOUT YOU

"Each of you should look not only to your own interests, but also to the interests of others."

Philippians 2:4 (BSB)

In the text, Paul challenges the Philippian church not to forget each other. It was important for Paul to encourage people to have each other's backs. One of my success steps in life was and is to let my soldiers know this: I have your backs, you can count on me, and you never walk alone. When the people you are leading know you care about them, they will go the extra mile for you. Plus, they see that your attitude is in the right place.

    I remember the 1982–1983 University of North Georgia basketball team was among the most exciting National Association of Intercollegiate Athletics (NAIA) teams in the nation that year. This team had the right balance of chemistry and talent to win back-to-back district championships. They were very unselfish and didn't care who got the credit.

This championship team was disciplined, daily exemplifying the United States Army's seven basic values on and off the court:

1. **Loyalty** They had each other's best interests at heart.
2. **Duty** They never had issues with doing their job.
3. **Respect** They treated each other with the utmost respect.
4. **Selfless Service** They put the team first. Therefore, they can look back and say they advanced to the national championship because they didn't care who got the credit.
5. **Honor** They had great respect for each other.
6. **Integrity** This team held each other accountable; therefore, they did the right thing regardless of the circumstances.
7. **Personal Courage** This team bounced back from adversity numerous times during the season. They are the only team in the University of North Georgia's history to have advanced to the NAIA National Championship because they understood there is no "I" in team, and they looked out for each other's interests.

Are you looking out for each other at your job? Are you looking out for each other in your marriage? Are you looking out for those who are less fortunate? Are you looking out for each other in your community?

DAY THIRTEEN

Remember, it's not all about you. Do not be a lone ranger.

APPLICATION

Answer these questions in a journal or notebook to reflect on today's devotional.

1. How have you shown compassion and care to your brothers and sisters?
2. What prevents you from showing God's love in your daily life?

> "Alone we can do so little; together we can do so much."
>
> **Hellen Keller**

STRENGTH FOR THE JOURNEY

Notes & Takeaways

In the space below, write your top three take-aways from this chapter.

DAY FOURTEEN

GREENER GRASS

"Keep your lives free from the love of money and be content with what you have."

Hebrews 13:5 (NIV)

Hebrews 13:5 says to be content in life and appreciate the things you have been blessed with. Never get so attached to material things that you desire what others have. In life, it's an easy temptation to envy someone else's life. We should be aware of and content with our gifts and abilities wherever life takes us.

The danger of discontentment is illustrated by the story of the cow who thought the grass was greener on the other side of the fence. In the story, two cows are in a field, separated by a fence. One cow said to the other cow, "Your grass is greener than mine. How do I get over to your side?" The cow eventually found a way to cross over the fence. The second cow said, "I hope you enjoy the green grass today because we eat on the green-grass side only once a week." The first cow responded, "I could eat green grass every day on the other side. Wow! I got what I wanted but lost what I had." The cow realized that what he had before was better than what he got on the other side of the fence.

God created each of us with unique gifts, and He has a unique plan for each of our lives. Only pursue what you know is right for you. That's the road to success—your road.

DAY FOURTEEN

APPLICATION

Answer these questions in a journal or notebook to reflect on today's devotional.

1. Why do we get trapped in thinking the grass is greener on the other side of the fence?
2. How might we learn contentment through Hebrews 13:5?

> *"Even if the grass is greener on the other side of the fence, keep to your own side; it's where you belong. There you can plant your own grass and tend to it."*
> **Richelle E. Goodrich**

STRENGTH FOR THE JOURNEY

Notes & Takeaways

In the space below, write your top three take-aways from this chapter.

DAY FIFTEEN

DIGGING IN

"May the God who gives endurance and encouragement give you the same attitude of mind toward each other that Christ had."

Romans 15:5 (NIV)

When I was stationed at Camp Greaves in Korea on the demilitarized zone (DMZ), I ran a seven-mile route every Friday with Kelvin Rankin, a company commander at Camp Greaves. The last two miles were a steep hill. We were running the hills to improve our speed, strength, and endurance. It seemed like Kelvin always knew exactly when to encourage me not to quit. Sometimes, I would say, "Kelvin, I don't think I will make it up the hill today."

He would look over and tell me, "You came too far to quit; you put too much effort in this run to quit." He would always say, "It's time for us to 'dig in.' Come on, Chaplain, we got to dig deep here." Once we dug in, we always made it to the top of that steep hill.

I want to encourage you not to focus on the steep hills in life but instead on getting to the finish line. No matter how steep the climb, there are times when we have to dig in. When burdens get heavy, dig in; when the night gets long, dig in. It may get tough when you are digging in and headed toward the finish line, but wait on God because He will dig in with you to cross the finish line.

Paul says, *"May the God who gives endurance and encouragement give you the same attitude of mind toward each other that Christ had."* Romans 15:5 (NIV).

God can give you the endurance you need to reach the finish line. As Kelvin would say, dig in, and you will get to the top of that steep hill in your life.

DAY FIFTEEN

APPLICATION

Answer these questions in a journal or notebook to reflect on today's devotional.

1. What areas in your life do you need to dig deeper into to overcome your obstacles?
2. Who can you encourage this week to endure and not quit when going up the steep hills in life?

"Whatever it is you are doing out there, don't lose hope, you just keep digging and things can work out. I am proof."
Carl Edwards

STRENGTH FOR THE JOURNEY

Notes & Takeaways

In the space below, write your top three take-aways from this chapter.

DAY SIXTEEN

NEVER SEEK REVENGE

"Do not seek revenge or bear a grudge against anyone among your people, but love your neighbor as yourself. I am the LORD."

Leviticus 19:18 (NIV)

Sometimes people can do the worst things to you, and if you're not careful, the only thing you'll think about is revenge. I remember when I was eight and my sister Maxine was seven. Our brother Charles sent us both a beautiful gift from Germany. Maxine received a beautiful music box with a man and woman dancing in the middle, and I received a fancy, state-of-the-art toy race car. Both gifts were one of a kind and could not be found anywhere in North Alabama. One day, my sister and I were playing with my car at our family's grocery store. I wound it up and let it rip. "Maxine," I said, "Here it comes. You need to catch it."

"Okay!" she said.

Maxine stepped aside instead as the car sped her

way, and the car hit the brick wall and smashed into pieces. I was so upset with my sister. She apologized, but I was determined to get revenge by destroying her gift. However, after looking at that beautiful music box, I could not damage it. I learned at an early age not to seek revenge or hold a grudge.

The author and psychologist Dr. Steven Stosny observes that vengeful people feel devalued by the hurt and betrayal they experience and try to feel more powerful through the adrenaline rush of revenge. While revenge can make them feel more powerful, it can never make them feel more valuable. Thus, revenge is never truly satisfying and is almost universally followed by either remorse or numbness. Consider finding value in showing compassion toward those who hurt you instead of going for the temporal rush of revenge. Leviticus 19:18 tells us not to hurt those who betray us, hurt us, or misuse us and never to hold grudges against people, but love them instead.

DAY SIXTEEN

APPLICATION

Answer these questions in a journal or notebook to reflect on today's devotional.

1. What is the life application of Leviticus 19:18 for your own life?
2. How do you work through not holding grudges and seeking revenge?

> *"That old law about 'an eye for an eye' leaves everybody blind. The time is always right to do the right thing."*
> **Dr. Martin Luther King Jr.**

STRENGTH FOR THE JOURNEY

Notes & Takeaways

In the space below, write your top three take-aways from this chapter.

DAY SEVENTEEN

GET OUT OF YOUR COMFORT ZONE

"For God has not given us a spirit of fear, but of power and of love and of a sound mind."

2 Timothy 1:7 (NKJV)

When I was in seminary, I remember one of the students sharing a story about a frog who fell into a pothole. The frog tried to get out of the hole, but he was comfortable after a while and stopped trying to escape. He ended up making a living there. One day, some of his friends were walking by and saw him in the pothole; they tried to get him out but couldn't. The frog told them, "It's cool. I'm okay. I got everything I need down here." So he continued making a home in the pothole. His friends tried again, but they failed. As they walked away, they heard a voice behind them; Mr. Frog was standing on the road. "How did you get out of that pothole?" said his friends. "Well, this is what happened," said the frog. "There was a big truck coming toward my pothole, and it was either me or that big truck. I got some hops that I didn't know I had, and that's how I caught up with you all."

Some of us are just like that frog who made his home in a pothole. We have gotten so comfortable that we are afraid to achieve something greater, but you can't chase your dreams or goals in a pothole. According to 2 Timothy 1:7 (NKJV), *"For God has not given us a spirit of fear, but of power and of love and of a sound mind."* God has given us all we need to pursue our dreams and goals.

Stop saying, "I can't do this" or "I can't do that." Stop listening to other people who are content with making their homes in potholes. God has given you a sound mind to think for yourself and see the not yet (your future) in the right now. In 2 Corinthians 12:9 (NIV), God said, *"My grace is sufficient for you, for my power is made perfect in weakness."* Remember, Bruce Wilkinson said, "It's when you begin to think about going to your dream that your dream is always outside of your comfort zone. It's always beyond what you've ever done."

DAY SEVENTEEN

APPLICATION

Answer these questions in a journal or notebook to reflect on today's devotional.

1. What potholes are you facing in life?
2. How can 2 Timothy 1:7 encourage you to deal with them?

> *"It's when you begin to think about going to your dream that your dream is always outside of your comfort zone. It's always beyond what you've ever done."*
>
> **Bruce Wilkinson**

STRENGTH FOR THE JOURNEY

Notes & Takeaways

In the space below, write your top three take-aways from this chapter.

DAY EIGHTEEN

A FATHER'S LOVE

"Jesus continued: "There was a man who had two sons. The younger one said to his father, Father, give me my share of the estate. So he divided his property between them. Not long after that, the younger son got together all he had, set off for a distant country and there squandered his wealth in wild living." "

Luke 11:13 (NIV)

From 1982 to 1984, I had an opportunity to play with John Dean, the best pure shooter to play at North Georgia College, now called North Georgia College and State University. John could shoot the basketball and knock it down from long range. He had a passion and love for basketball that was second to none. He also had an excellent work ethic and always worked hard on his shooting skills. John used that same passion, love, and commitment in raising his two boys, Brandon and Jacques Dean. After thirty-seven years, I caught up with John and had the opportunity to meet his two well-mannered boys. John shared with me how he had been involved in their life since infants. No matter what they decided to do, he supported and encouraged them to be the best at whatever they chose to participate in.

John taught his boys to treat everyone with dignity and respect. He would take his boys to church and discuss the lesson from the weekly service with them. He instilled in them that he would never forsake or leave them if they made mistakes. They could always trust him to be there for them. His boys are now young adults, but John is still in their life to coach, teach, and mentor them whenever they need guidance. John is still demonstrating "A Father's Love" to his boys. He has been a great role model to his boys, and he loves them unconditionally.

I am reminded of the story of the Prodigal Son in Luke 15. The younger son wasted his living and ended up living in a hog pen, so he decided to return to his Father's house. He said, "I am no longer worthy of being called your son; make me like one of your hired servants." The story ended with his father restoring him and celebrating his return. No matter what you are going through or how many times you have fallen, we have a Father who loves us and welcomes our return. He loves us unconditionally. No matter where we find ourselves in life, He will be there, waiting for us when we return to him. The Isaacs family wrote: "I cannot make a world and hold it in my hands; I cannot make the lightening flash across the land; I cannot take a piece of clay and mold it into man; But I have a father, I have a father who can."

DAY EIGHTEEN

APPLICATION

Answer this question in a journal or notebook to reflect on today's devotional.

Can you recall a time when you experienced God's unconditional love?

"A father's love is eternal and without end."
Amy Hoover

STRENGTH FOR THE JOURNEY

Notes & Takeaways

In the space below, write your top three take-aways from this chapter.

DAY NINETEEN

GOD IS WATCHING OVER YOU

"'What is the price of two sparrows—one copper coin? But not a single sparrow can fall to the ground without your Father knowing it.'"

Matthew 10:29 (NLT)

God notices every time a little bird falls from the sky. Don't you know He sees and knows the things we are going through?

I heard a story about a group of ladies who visited a goldsmith; they were curious about how he handled gold. They asked him to explain the process to them. He said, "Sure, what I do is put the gold in a smelting pot, then I turn the fire on under the pot." The ladies then asked if he did other things while the gold was cooking. He said, "No, as a matter of fact, when the gold is cooking, I watch it more closely than at any other time because if it overcooks and will damage the gold." Don't you know God is watching us closely when we go through our trials and tribulations because He knows just how much we can bear? Remember, God checks in on the birds and knows when one is falling from the sky. So He is indeed watching over you when you go through tough times. There is a song that says, "His eye is on the sparrow, and I know He watches over me."

The ladies then asked how he knew when the gold was ready. Mr. Goldsmith replied, "That is easy; when I can look over in the pot and see my reflection, I know the gold is ready." When God can see His reflection in our lives, He knows that we are ready to "run and not be weary" and "walk and not faint." Another song says, "Please be patient with me because God is not through with me yet. When God gets through with me, I will come forth as pure gold."

DAY NINETEEN

APPLICATION

Answer these questions in a journal or notebook to reflect on today's devotional.

1. How does it encourage you to know that God is watching over you?
2. How has God sustained you when you felt alone?

"If God is watching your every move, you should probably straighten up your act a little bit."
— Misha Collins

STRENGTH FOR THE JOURNEY

Notes & Takeaways

In the space below, write your top three take-aways from this chapter.

DAY TWENTY

INCOMING! INCOMING!

"Those who live in the shelter of the Most High will find rest in the shadow of the Almighty. This I declare about the Lord: He alone is my refuge, my place of safety; he is my God, and I trust Him."

Psalm 91:1-2 (NLT)

If you have ever been to Iraq or Afghanistan, you are familiar with the sound of a siren going off, followed by a voice saying these words over the microphone: "Incoming! Incoming! IDE (Rocket Attack) in progress. Take cover." One night at a particular Forward Operating Base (FOB) in Afghanistan, we were hit by about twelve rockets. My Noncommissioned Officer in Charge (NCOIC) Sergeant First Class (SFC), Robert Blalock, now a Sergeant Major, acted very swiftly and led me to the bunker. He not only guided me but also hovered over me to make sure I was safe. He said, "Sir, any incoming rocket has to hit me first before it hits you." I thought about that years later. Robert put his life on the line to protect me from all the incoming rockets.

We are constantly facing incoming rockets in the form of stress, pressure, grief, loss, and obstacles. Accidents will arise, and incoming tragedies will happen. Who protects you from all of these incoming trials and tribulations?

God said He would protect you from these incoming hardships if you trust Him. *"Those who live in the shelter of the Most High will find rest in the shadow of the Almighty. This I declare about the Lord: He alone is my refuge, my place of safety; he is my God, and I trust Him"* Psalm 91:1-2 (NLT). God will pull you out of the miry clay and plant your feet on the rock to stay. God is your safe haven when the siren goes off, He will be your Bunker in the times of a storm, covering you from all incoming trials and tribulations.

DAY TWENTY

APPLICATION

Answer these questions in a journal or notebook to reflect on today's devotional.

1. Read Psalm 91 and meditate on it throughout the week.
2. How has God enabled you to handle all of your problems when the siren goes off in your life?

> *"If God be our God, He will give us peace in trouble. When there is a storm without, He will make peace within. The world can create trouble in peace, but God can create peace in trouble."*
> **Thomas Watson**

STRENGTH FOR THE JOURNEY

Notes & Takeaways

In the space below, write your top three take-aways from this chapter.

DAY TWENTY-ONE

LOOKING ON THE POSITIVE SIDE

"Let all bitterness and wrath and anger and clamor and slander be put away from you, along with all malice. Be kind to one another, tenderhearted, forgiving one another, as God in Christ forgave you."

Ephesians 4:31-32 (ESV)

It has been said that "your attitude affects your altitude," which means that you will go as far as your attitude in life. I worked with a young lady at Fort Riley who I never saw have a bad day. Judy Woodward was the Health Promotion Officer, and she had the perfect attitude in guiding our Health Promotion Council Board. There were so many different attitudes to deal with, but I watched how Judy chose the right attitude every time to accomplish our mission. The task sometimes looked impossible, yet she never complained. Even when the group complained, she would say, "Let's meet and figure out how to get the mission done." Judy always looked at the positive side of life. Judy's attitude reminds me of a story I heard about two buckets who went to the well to draw water.

One bucket said to the other bucket, "It breaks my heart that no matter how full we leave the well, we always come back empty."

The other bucket replied, "I look at the positive side. No matter how empty we come back to the well, we always leave full."

Whether you believe it or not, our attitudes impact our environment, our lives, and the lives of others. We need to choose an attitude that will change our setting for the better and bring harmony to those around us. As Viktor Frankl, a Nazi death camp survivor, once said, "Everything can be taken away from a [person] but one thing: the last of the human freedoms—to choose one's attitude in any given set of circumstances."

Paul said that if you want to have the right attitude, then *"Let all bitterness and wrath and anger and clamor and slander be put away from you, along with all malice. Be kind to one another, tenderhearted, forgiving one another, as God in Christ forgave you."* Ephesians 4:31-32 (ESV).

DAY TWENTY-ONE

APPLICATION

Answer this question in a journal or notebook to reflect on today's devotional.

What is your strategy of maintaining a positive attitude when working around negative people?

> *"If you can stay positive in a negative situation, you win."*
>
> **Anonymous**

STRENGTH FOR THE JOURNEY

Notes & Takeaways

In the space below, write your top three take-aways from this chapter.

DAY TWENTY-TWO

ALL IN!

"I have fought the good fight, I have finished the race, I have kept the faith."

2 Timothy 4:7 (NKJV)

How many times have you heard the phrase "all in"? Whether you hear these words from a coach, commander, teacher, supervisor, or family member, to be "all in" means to be fully committed to a cause, no matter how many setbacks you have. The Apostle Paul, after his Damascus experience, is an excellent example of someone who is all in. He was fully committed to the task before him. Many of us don't like committing ourselves to a task that requires too much time and energy. We are okay with just going through life, contributing every now and then, but stopping short of commitment.

I am reminded of a story I heard called "The Pig and the Chicken." In the story, the chicken said to the pig, "I had a great idea this morning."

"Let me hear it," said the pig.

"Our owner has been so good to us," said the chicken. "He is always there for us and makes sure we have what we need. Let's make him some ham and eggs this morning."

The pig hesitated and didn't immediately respond to the chicken.

The chicken said, "Did I say something wrong?"

The pig said, "You will only make a contribution and lay a few eggs, but you are asking me to be all in and make the ultimate sacrifice."

Like the chicken in the story, some of us make only a few contributions to our work, marriage, kids, community, and church. However, you need to be committed to some things in life if you want to be effective and successful. No matter how much time or energy you have to exert, you need to stay focused and be all in to chase your dreams. Whatever you are assigned, own it and do it with excellence. In 2 Timothy 4:7, Paul tells us that he was all in, and through the good times and bad times he had "fought the good fight, finished his race, and kept the faith."

DAY TWENTY-TWO

APPLICATION

Reflect on 2 Timothy 4:7 and write down examples of what it means to be all in from your point of view.

> *"You cannot conquer what you are not committed to."*
>
> **T.D. Jakes**

STRENGTH FOR THE JOURNEY

Notes & Takeaways

In the space below, write your top three take-aways from this chapter.

DAY TWENTY-THREE

SPIRITUAL IMMATURITY

"And I, brethren, could not speak to you as to spiritual people but as to carnal, as to babes in Christ. I fed you with milk and not with solid food; for until now you were not able to receive it, and even now you are still not able."

I Corinthians 3:1-2 (NKJV)

In 1 Corinthians 3:1-3, Paul addresses the church on spiritual immaturity. He says they are self-centered crybabies who are impatient, helpless, noisy, messy, and still holding grudges against one another. Hint, hint! Some people never grow spiritually: they read their Bibles, do daily devotionals, attend prayer meetings, and, of course, go to church on Sunday; then, on Monday, you have to be careful how you handle them. Grandmama used to say that if you say the wrong thing to these people, they will fly off the handle. No matter how hard you work with them, some folks continue to walk in immaturity.

My dad had several businesses, and in his spare time, he would raise animals. One time, I remember a sow delivering a litter of pigs. We fed the piglets every day, but four or five of them did not grow as time went by. I said, "Dad, what happened here?" And he said, "Son, nothing happened. Now and then, it happens that some of them just don't reach maturity. They are called runts." So now, when I see grown people throwing a temper tantrum and not speaking because things didn't go their way, I see immature runts because they reject any advice that encourages them to lay the past aside and move on with their lives.

Paul is saying you should be mature, past that now, and growing in the faith. There is no way you can fulfill your God-given responsibilities unless you lay aside your spiritual immaturity.

DAY TWENTY-THREE

APPLICATION

Answer these questions in a journal or notebook to reflect on today's devotional.

1. How do you respond when someone points out that you made the wrong plans?
2. How can you respond humbly as a mature person?
3. What are your thoughts on 1 Corinthians 3:1–2?

"Spiritual maturity does not mean that we will never make wrong plans. In fact, spiritual maturity often means having the courage to admit we've made the wrong plans."
Beth Moore

STRENGTH FOR THE JOURNEY

Notes & Takeaways

In the space below, write your top three take-aways from this chapter.

DAY TWENTY-FOUR

GOD IS YOUR FRONT-WHEEL DRIVE

"'You of little faith, why are you so afraid?'"
Matthew 8:26 (NIV)

I remember when my uncle Bobby took me to Nashville on a basketball recruiting trip in 1979. My mother didn't want him to take me on that particular day because the weather was terrible. It had snowed the night before, and the snow had turned into ice by the early morning. However, Uncle Bobby was still willing to take us. He told Mother not to worry because we would be in a front-wheel-drive (FWD) that would make it through the snow and patches of ice. He said the key is not to get stuck in the ice. So we hit I-65 North, and we were on our way. We hadn't gotten far before we saw other cars beginning to pull over. Mother said to her brother, "If you want to pull over and turn around, it's okay because all these other cars have gotten stuck." He kept going. We went a little further and saw that more cars had pulled over. Mother said, "We may need to turn around."

Uncle said, "Don't worry, this is a front-wheel drive, and we are getting good traction on the snow." He explained that an FWD was more suited for rugged terrain and snow. Finally, we made it to our destination. Uncle Bobby told us that if we had pulled over, we would still be stuck in the snowstorm with the other vehicles that had pulled over.

In life, some things will rock your world. It may not just rock your world but turn it upside down, but there is no time to pull over. You have to push through the storm. God is your front-wheel drive, and He can navigate you through the storms of your life. No matter what you are going through, God will give you the traction to get through it.

The disciples were also afraid when a storm came upon their ship. Jesus said in Matthew 8:26 (NIV), *"You of little faith, why are you so afraid?"* Then He got up and rebuked the winds and the waves, and they became completely calm. God is our front-wheel drive, and He doesn't mind how many times we call upon Him. He will see us through our storms.

DAY TWENTY-FOUR

APPLICATION

Answer these questions in a journal or notebook to reflect on today's devotional.

1. Why do we sometimes make the mistake of parking during storms in our life?
2. How can you trust God to take control of your storms and bring you through them?

> *"Never make a permanent decision based on a temporary storm. No matter how raging the billows are today, remind yourself: 'This too shall pass!'"*
>
> **T.D. Jakes**

STRENGTH FOR THE JOURNEY

Notes & Takeaways

In the space below, write your top three take-aways from this chapter.

DAY TWENTY-FIVE

MAKING A COMEBACK

"What then shall we say to these things? If God is for us, who can be against us?"

Romans 8:31 (ESV)

Tony Grossi wrote a story in the Plain Dealer Reporter on November 4, 2001, titled "A Stunner and a Bummer." It was the story of a game between the Cleveland Browns and the Chicago Bears. With only twenty-eight seconds remaining, the Browns led 21 to 7. The Browns were packed up and ready to go home when the Bears scored, making the game 21 to 14. The Bears then recovered their onside kick and threw a Hail Mary pass, resulting in another touchdown tying the game at 21 to 21. The game went into overtime, and two minutes and forty-three seconds later, the Bears intercepted a Browns pass and ran it back for a touchdown. The Bears won 28 to 21. The Bears scored two touchdowns in twenty-eight seconds and a third touchdown in overtime to move a

21 to 7 deficit to a 28 to 21 win. A football game like this is an image for life. It teaches us that you can make a comeback no matter how far you are behind in life.

A new year brings new opportunities. It's a time for a fresh start. We make new year resolutions that we will do things differently, but most of us break those resolutions within a few months. If we are not careful, the new year begins to look like the old year. However, the new year allows us to make a comeback from what has set us back last year. Most people love to see the underdog make a comeback. Have you ever made a comeback? Do you know of anyone who has made a comeback? Some of us may have fallen behind last year and never recovered. We have a new year to make a comeback and overcome those obstacles that caused us to stumble last year.

Some of us are on the journey to make a comeback from fear, loneliness, depression, guilt, shame, abandonment, grief, prejudice, heartache, pains, etc. I don't care where you are on the road to recovery; never give up. With God on your side, you can make a comeback in this new year. The Bible says, *"If God is for us, who can be against us?"* Romans 8:31 (ESV). If God is on our side, there is no need to fear anyone while trying to make a comeback. If God is on our side, there is no need to be afraid of any obstacles we may face in making our comeback. If God is for us, He will not abandon us on the road to our comeback. This is

DAY TWENTY-FIVE

your year to make a comeback because God is setting you up for a great comeback story.

APPLICATION

Answer this question in a journal or notebook to reflect on today's devotional.

> What obstacles do you need to overcome to make a comeback in the new year?

> *"To have a comeback, you have to have a setback."*
>
> **Mr. T**

STRENGTH FOR THE JOURNEY

Notes & Takeaways

In the space below, write your top three take-aways from this chapter.

DAY TWENTY-SIX

A FRIEND THAT STICKS CLOSER THAN A BROTHER

"One who has unreliable friends soon comes to ruin, but there is a friend who sticks closer than a brother."

Proverbs 18:24 (NIV)

A genuine friendship is a bond between two persons loyal to each other. Bennie Harris, an Auburn fan, and Charles Lockhart, an Alabama fan, were born in 1948 in Madison County, Alabama. At a young age, they made a covenant to everlasting friendship. Bennie and Charles cared about each other like brothers. They spent time with each other growing up, playing sports, fishing, shooting marbles, and watching football and basketball. You hardly saw one without the other. They always had each other's back. They could count on each other and knew the other person would be there. They have one of the most committed friendships I have ever seen. They were like family, and if you didn't know them, you would think they were brothers. The friendship is so genuine that it's easy to see and feel their affection for each other. Even today, when their friends or relatives see one without the other, right away, they hear the phrase where is your "sidekick." I don't know of anything appreciated, blessed, and more inspiring than a true friend.

I noticed three things that made Bennie and Charles friends that stick closer than a brother:

> **A friend is committed.** They are so tight that even when they were job hunting as young men, they would look out for each other.
>
> **A friend chooses to love always.** No matter what they were faced with, love always kept them close friends.
>
> **A friend is trustworthy.** They always trust and lean on each other during hard times. They have been there for each other through the good and bad times.

Even as close as Bennie and Charles are, there is someone who will stick even closer than a brother. Jesus is a friend that sticks closer than a brother.

The Bible says, *"One who has unreliable friends soon comes to ruin, but there is a friend who sticks closer than a brother."* Proverbs 18:24 (NIV). This scripture is saying those we consider reliable will soon let us down, but Jesus is a friend that will stick closer than a brother. He will be there when everyone else walks

DAY TWENTY-SIX

away. He will stick close to us when the circumstances turn against us. He will stick closer to us when we are going through the valley and "walking through the shadow of death." When we accept Jesus as our friend, we can be assured He will never forsake us. He is the only friend I know who is so committed that He laid his life down for us.

APPLICATION

Jesus is extending His hands out today and saying, "Let me be a friend that will stick closer than a brother." *Will you accept his friendship?*

> *"A friend is someone who understands your past, believes in your future, and accepts you just the way you are."*
> **Unknown**

STRENGTH FOR THE JOURNEY

Notes & Takeaways

In the space below, write your top three take-aways from this chapter.

DAY TWENTY-SEVEN

DON'T BE SCARED

"The LORD is my light and my salvation; whom shall I fear? the LORD is the strength of my life; of whom shall I be afraid?"

Psalm 27:1 (KJV)

Don't be scared. Don't be scared. The first time I heard that phrase was watching one of my favorite movies, Life, starring Eddie Murphy as Ray and Martin Lawrence as Claud. Ray and Claud were sentenced to life in a prison in Mississippi for a crime they didn't commit. Ray wanted to make sure he got his bluff in early upon arrival to prevent any confrontation with him and Claud. One day while at lunch, this big bully looked at Claud and said, "Do you want your cornbread?" Claud, of course, didn't want any trouble, so he got ready to give his cornbread up. Ray did not want Claud to go out like a wimp because he knew if he gave up his cornbread this time, he would have to give it up the next time and the next time. It would never end. So, Ray said, "No, he is not giving up his cornbread."

Suddenly, Ray and this big bully were out in the yard throwing down in a fight. Ray didn't stand a chance at winning. He got the beat down and was left tore up from the floor up. Claud stood there looking at how his friend had been beaten down over some cornbread. He stood there evidently with the look of fear on his face when one of the prison brothers walked up to him, and he said, "Claud, don't be scared; don't be scared." Someone is reading this devotional who needs to hear these same words. Don't be scared! Don't be scared!

The next time you are faced with making a difficult decision or pressured into something that challenges your integrity, pause and reflect on Psalm 27:1. This Psalm teaches us that God is our light, the strength of our life, and we don't have to be scared. Don't be scared! No matter how heavy the burden, how dark the valley, or how long the night, God is our light and our strength; He will fight our battles.

DAY TWENTY-SEVEN

APPLICATION

Answer these questions in a journal or notebook to reflect on today's devotional.

1. Write down your thoughts about some of the things that cause you to be scared?
2. How can you apply Psalm 27:1 to assert your faith and calm your fears so you can deal with the things that scare you?

> *"Never be bullied into silence. Never allow yourself to be made a victim. Accept no one's definition of your life, but define yourself."*
> **Harvey Fierstein**

STRENGTH FOR THE JOURNEY

Notes & Takeaways

In the space below, write your top three take-aways from this chapter.

DAY TWENTY-EIGHT

A LESSON IN HUMILITY

"Likewise you younger people, submit yourselves to your elders. Yes, all of you be submissive to one another, and be clothed with humility, for 'God resists the proud, But gives grace to the humble.' Therefore, humble yourselves under the mighty hand of God, that He may exalt you in due time, casting all your care upon Him, for He cares for you."

I Peter 5:5-7 (NKJV)

According to Merriam-Webster, the essential meaning of humility is the quality or state of not thinking you are better than other people: the quality or state of being humble. We don't talk about the word humility much. There is too much pride going on in the world today. People think you have to step on and over people to obtain success. The word humility has been on my mind all week.

I can't think of anyone who embodies this word more than my good friend Willie Thomas. I had an opportunity to play two years with Willie at North Georgia College, now called North Georgia College and State University. Willie was the star player on the basketball team. He was named college player of the year in Georgia and named to the NAIA All American

Basketball team. In 2012, Willie Thomas was inducted into the North Georgia College and State University Athletics Hall of Fame. You would never have known it by his character. He never once mentioned to us how good he was, never put All American on his tennis shoes, and never wore a shirt showcasing being named college player of the year in the state of Georgia. He was so down to earth and the most humble person I have ever met. He was confident but not arrogant. Can you imagine what kind of world we would have if more individuals showed humility to all people like Willie Thomas did?

I Peter 5:5 says, *"Be clothed with humility."* The opposite of humility is pride. The Bible says, *"Pride goes before destruction, And a haughty spirit before a fall."* Proverbs 16:18 (NKJV). Pride is an evil spirit and the devil's trap to bring his victims down. As you observe, you will often realize that most people struggling with pride are not content with their lives. So they go around being haughty or puffed up, yet the people who God lifted are humble because they recognized their elevation comes from God. That's the secret of true humility. Consider 1 Peter 5:6, *"Therefore humble yourselves under the mighty hand of God, that He may exalt you in due time."* Humility is a prerequisite for God lifting us.

DAY TWENTY-EIGHT

PRAYER

Dear God,
Help us understand that humility is a kingdom secret and a prerequisite for you to take us to realms and heights beyond our wildest dreams. Help us appreciate humility as an attitude we should willingly adopt. In Jesus' name, amen.

APPLICATION

How does one change their attitude and become a humble servant? It's a choice. Otherwise, God would have never commanded that we humble ourselves.

> *"Humility will open more doors than arrogance ever will."*
> **Zig Ziglar**

STRENGTH FOR THE JOURNEY

Notes & Takeaways

In the space below, write your top three take-aways from this chapter.

DAY TWENTY-NINE

RESTORING HOPE TO BROKEN DREAMS

"And let us not grow weary of doing good, for in due season we will reap, if we do not give up."

Galatians 6:9 (ESV)

This week, after looking at the movie Life again, I kept looking for the reason Claud was so afraid. Evidently, there was a message being relayed from that brother to Claud, who had found himself in a situation that he didn't want to be in. Claud's fear possibly erupted because of the situation he found himself in; he had no control over it. If we keep living, all of us will find ourselves caught up in a situation that we don't have control over, and fear may grip us. Why? You are caught up in something that challenges your integrity. Once fear grips you, if you allow it to remain too long, you become enslaved to it. Maybe Claud feared that his dreams had been shattered. When you have a dream you want to fulfill, and things don't happen as you planned, you could easily condition yourself to live a life of fear. Some of us get scared when we are diverted from our comfort zone.

What was Claud's dream? Claud had gotten a job as a New York banker. He dreamed of moving up in banking and marrying his girlfriend. That was Claud's dream in life, but that dream was shattered. Maybe your dreams have not panned out, and you have started downsizing them, limiting what you had anticipated for your life. Why? It didn't go right the last time; perhaps you don't think it will go right the next time, and you are allowing your dreams to dry up. However, the good news is this: Galatians 6:9 says, *"And let us not grow weary of doing good, for in due season we will reap, if we do not give up."* If we stay focused on our dreams and don't give up, our dreams will be fulfilled in due season. God is trustworthy in every situation; He is the mender of our broken dreams. Never forget God can, and God will restore hope to broken dreams.

DAY TWENTY-NINE

APPLICATION

Answer these questions in a journal or notebook to reflect on today's devotional.

1. Take a moment, and list your broken dreams.
2. How can you apply Galatians 6:9 to get re-energized and pursue your dreams?

Hold fast to dreams, for if dreams die, life is a broken-winged bird that cannot fly."
Langston Hughes

STRENGTH FOR THE JOURNEY

Notes & Takeaways

In the space below, write your top three take-aways from this chapter.

DAY THIRTY

THIS CHAPTER IS OVER

"Brethren, I do not count myself to have apprehended; but one thing I do, forgetting those things which are behind and reaching forward to those things which are ahead, I press toward the goal for the prize of the upward call of God in Christ Jesus."
Philippians 3:13-14 (NKJV)

Paul was putting behind all the things that hindered his walk with God. In other words, he was saying that it was God who had enabled him to overcome his past life, forgiven him, and erased the memories that were paralyzing him. Paul understood he could not let the past control his future. He is saying to us today, "This chapter is over."

It doesn't matter what you went through last year; that chapter is over. No more re-run relationships and no more misuse and abuse; that chapter is over.

I went to Sparkman High in Toney, Alabama. We had a great basketball team back in the day. After we'd destroyed our opponents, with only minutes left in the game, our home crowd would stand up and start singing, "Na, na, na,na, hey, hey, hey, goodbye." When your past comes calling trying to interfere with your future, you need to say, "Na, na, na, na, hey, hey, hey, goodbye." This chapter is over. Don't take your old issues into a new year. If you do, the year will begin to look like the last one all over again.

Paul went on to say, "Reach for the things which are ahead." He was reaching for the perfection of knowledge, holiness, and happiness, which were before him. This year, we should strive to walk closer with God, seeking after his favor. Paul said, "Run to win; give it all you've got."

We need to remember what Shakespeare said, "There is a divinity that shapes our end." Let me break it down: Shakespeare simply said that when you go through stuff that is out of your control, God is still in control. So forget those things from the past and reach for the things before you. This chapter is over; it is time to write a new one.

DAY THIRTY

APPLICATION

Make a list of the things in your past that you need to move on from/ let go of. This is your year, so stay focused on your dreams and goals!

> *"The new year stands before us, like a chapter in a book, waiting to be written."*
>
> **Melody Beattie**

STRENGTH FOR THE JOURNEY

Notes & Takeaways

In the space below, write your top three take-aways from this chapter.

DAY THIRTY-ONE

TRUST GOD WHEN YOU CAN'T TRACE HIM

"Trust in the LORD with all your heart, And lean not on your own understanding; In all your ways acknowledge Him, And He shall direct your paths."

Proverbs 3:5-6 (NKJV)

I f you're honest with yourself, there are times when you can't trace the presence of God in your life. Sometimes life will drive you to the point where it makes no sense, and you are trusting God to deliver you. God, where are you? God, when are you going to show up in my life? I have not heard from you in a long time. God, are you still with me? I used to trace small victories from you, and I could see you were walking along with me. Now, God, I can't trace you anywhere in my life. You said you would be with me, but I am in this storm by myself and can't see my way out. Are you feeling like that today? If so, be encouraged because Proverbs 3:5-6 (NKJV) says, *"Trust in the LORD with all your heart, And lean not on your own understanding; In all your ways acknowledge Him, And He shall direct your paths."*

When you can't trace God, continue to trust him. Remember the poem "Footprints in the Sand"? "One night, I dreamed a dream as I was walking along the beach with my Lord. Across the dark sky flashed scenes from my life. For each scene, I noticed two sets of footprints in the sand, one belonging to me and one to my Lord. After the last scene of my life flashed before me, I looked back at the footprints in the sand. I noticed that there was only one set of footprints at many times along the path of my life, especially at the very lowest and saddest times.

This really troubled me, so I asked the Lord about it. 'Lord, you said once I decided to follow you, you'd walk with me all the way. But I noticed that there was only one set of footprints during the saddest and most troublesome times of my life. I don't understand why, when I needed You the most, You would leave me.' He whispered, 'My precious child, I love you and will never leave you. Never, ever, during your trials and testing. When you saw only one set of footprints, it was then that I carried you.'" Keep following as God directs your path and trust Him when you can't trace Him; He is there to carry you.

DAY THIRTY-ONE

APPLICATION

Complete these items in a journal or notebook to reflect on today's devotional.

1. Take a moment and list times when you could not trace God, but He provided for you.
2. How can you apply Proverbs 3:5-6 to help you, your family, or your friends get through difficult times of your life?

> *"God is God. He knows what he is doing. When you can't trace His hand, trust His heart."*
> **Max Lucado**

STRENGTH FOR THE JOURNEY

Notes & Takeaways

In the space below, write your top three take-aways from this chapter.

DAY THIRTY-TWO

YOU CAN'T PLEASE EVERYBODY

"Am I now trying to win the approval of human beings, or of God? Or am I trying to please people? If I were still trying to please people, I would not be a servant of Christ."
Galatians 1:10 (NIV)

A few weeks ago, I saw a young lady wearing a t-shirt with the saying, "I Am Who I Am. Your Approval Is Not Needed." I thought about Galatians 1:10 because we have to understand that we don't need anyone else's approval to make the right decision if we walk with God. When you seek the approval of others, you will end up carrying that donkey on your back.

An old story tells about an older man traveling with a boy and a donkey. As they walked through a village, the man led the donkey, and the boy walked behind. The townspeople said the older man was a fool for not riding, so to please them, he climbed up on the animal's back. When they came to the next village, the people said the older man was cruel to let the child walk while he enjoyed the ride. So, to please them, he got off, sat the boy on the animal's back, and continued on his way. In the third village, people accused the child of being lazy for making the older man walk, and the suggestion was made that they both ride. So the man climbed on, and they set off again. Finally, they came to a fourth village, and the townspeople were indignant at the cruelty to the donkey because he was made to carry two people. The frustrated man was last seen going down the road carrying the donkey on his back.

As ridiculous as this story sounds, the point made is a good one: You can't please everybody. If you live your life trying, you'll end up carrying the donkey of frustration, discouragement, and indecisiveness.

DAY THIRTY-TWO

APPLICATION

God,
We seek to follow the best course of action here in our lives; we know there will be others who are quick to find fault and offer criticism. However, please give us the strength of character to do what is right in your sight, regardless of what other people do or think. "We had a purpose before anyone had an opinion." Always do what is right in your heart.

"Be happy. Be yourself. If others don't like it, then let them be. Happiness is a choice. Life isn't about pleasing everybody."
John Spencer

STRENGTH FOR THE JOURNEY

Notes & Takeaways

In the space below, write your top three take-aways from this chapter.

DAY THIRTY-THREE

WHAT IS YOUR VISION?

"Write the vision And make it plain on tablets, That he may run who reads it."

Habakkuk 2:2 (NKJV)

Habakkuk said God spoke and told him to write the vision and make it plain that when folks are walking by, they can see it and then run with it.

What is a vision? A vision is God giving you a preview of a coming attraction. A vision is when you receive a revelation that is greater than your current situation. Many of you wanted this year to be your year, but you didn't have a vision. How do you expect your life to have meaning when you are just going through the motions every day? God will give you a purpose. He will provide you with a preview of what is possible, and once you know what is possible, you cannot be content with the present because you know greater is possible. After all, you know that you got a greater future tense than your present tense. You need a vision to set yourself up for victory, no matter how bad your vicissitudes are. Once you get a vision, that vision orders your steps. That vision dictates your direction, and that direction dictates your priority. Now your priority focuses on your vision. You keep moving toward your vision because your passion motivates you to stay enthusiastic about vision.

When McDonald's has a vision to build a new restaurant, it may take a year or two before that vision comes to fruition. One day while passing by, you see a sign that says McDonald's coming soon. That is just the end goal of the vision developed months ago. The next time someone asks you when you will see your vision come to fruition, tell them it is coming soon. Keep moving in the direction of the vision because the best is yet to come; the worst has already happened. Place your vision in plain view to be read each day.

DAY THIRTY-THREE

APPLICATION

Complete these items in a journal or notebook to reflect on today's devotional.

1. Write down your short-term and long-term vision for your life. Are you on track? If not, what do you need to do to get back on track?
2. Read Habakkuk 2:2 and write down your thoughts on how this verse can help you with purpose, direction, and motivation.

> *"The only thing worse than being blind is having sight but no vision."*
>
> **Helen Keller**

STRENGTH FOR THE JOURNEY

Notes & Takeaways

In the space below, write your top three take-aways from this chapter.

DAY THIRTY-FOUR

DON'T TAP OUT

"And He said to me, 'My grace is sufficient for you, for My strength is made perfect in weakness.'"

2 Corinthians 12:9 (NKJV)

Paul had been afflicted. A thorn in the flesh had attacked him. It was a painful experience, and he asked God three times to remove it. Paul truly felt like tapping out. I don't care who you are; all of us know something about life being so painful that all we can do is turn to God and beg for some kind of relief. At that moment, we want to tap out and give up.

I remember the young man who won a wrestling championship against all odds. He was undersized, and therefore, he was the underdog. In his last match against the two-time defending champ, he was getting beaten badly. At one point, the pain was so unbearable that he almost tapped out. However, he suddenly got some strength and won the match against all odds. Later, he was asked, "Why didn't you tap out?" He said,

"My dad was watching and said, 'Son, don't tap out. You got this.'" That gave him the strength to overcome the pain that his opponent had inflicted on him. Though the pain was still there, he gained strength from his dad's words, which encouraged him not to tap out.

God was really saying, "Paul, don't tap out. I will not remove the thorn, but I will put my arms of grace and protection around you. The pain will still be there, but Paul, my grace is sufficient for you, and my strength is made perfect in weakness."

The next time you feel like giving up, the next time someone says you will not make it, the next time your friends walk away from you, the next time you have to endure painful and hurtful moments, remember that God's grace is sufficient for you. No matter what your situation, don't tap out.

DAY THIRTY-FOUR

APPLICATION

Complete these items in a journal or notebook to reflect on today's devotional.

1. Take a moment and list times when you felt like tapping out, but God provided for you.
2. Read 2 Corinthians 12:9, and identify how this scripture encourages you, family, and friends not to tap out.

> *"Never let success get to your head. Never let failure get to your heart."*
>
> **Anonymous**

STRENGTH FOR THE JOURNEY

Notes & Takeaways

In the space below, write your top three take-aways from this chapter.

DAY THIRTY-FIVE

EXTENDING GRACE

"For I was hungry and you gave Me food; I was thirsty and you gave Me drink; I was a stranger and you took Me in; I was naked and you clothed Me; I was sick and you visited Me; I was in prison and you came to Me."
                                    Matthew 25:35-36:20 (NKJV)

God is such a gracious God, and he is constantly extending grace to us. He always gives us favor, blessings, and kindness even when we don't deserve it. If we ever understand what God's grace is all about, we will see lasting transformation in our communities. Jeanie Ames, a good friend of mine, understands what God's grace is all about. Jeanie is a registered nurse (RN) I met in Manhattan, KS, in 2007. I met Jeanie a few days after my lung surgery. Jeanie extended grace to me during my recovery, but I was more impressed as I got to know her better. Jeanie is a devout Catholic who understands what God's Grace is all about. Jeanie has extended grace to those she served throughout her career without discrimination; regardless of color, religion, or country of origin, she served anyone in need wholeheartedly. She has ministered to women experiencing domestic violence through counseling., additionally she visited patients in nursing homes. As a former patient of Jeanie Ames, I vividly remember how Jeanie extended grace to all her patients regardless of their positions in society.

From Mathew 25:35-36, we learn that doing good to people is not necessarily because they deserve it, nor should it be only because they have done us well and we are trying to pay them back. On the contrary, the scripture in reference challenges us to extend grace sometimes to total strangers like those in prison, hospitals, or someone in dire need. Have you ever thought of taking time out of your busy schedule to visit the sick and shut-in? This is just an example; let's be determined to extend grace and change lives. In this month, as we honor women, we can emulate women like Jeanie Ames by remembering that the workplace; is our marketplace where God can use us to minister to the people, we serve by similarly extending grace without any discrimination.

PRAYER

Dear God,

Please constantly remind us by your spirit to love others as we love ourselves; in that way, we will not hurt but help improve communities for your glory.

DAY THIRTY-FIVE

APPLICATION

One of the greatest fulfillments in this life is seeing lives changed, yet more fulfilling is being part of their story of positively changing their lives. How can you deliberately position yourself to be the change vehicle in the lives of those disadvantaged or less fortunate in your community?

> *"I can survive in the jungle, so now I can do anything."*
>
> **Emily Atack**

STRENGTH FOR THE JOURNEY

Notes & Takeaways

In the space below, write your top three take-aways from this chapter.

DAY THIRTY-SIX

WALK BY FAITH

"For we walk by faith, not by sight."
2 *Corinthians* 5:7 *(NKJV)*

As long as we can see it, touch it, or feel it, we are okay. As long as it is in the bank account, everything is fine. When we can't see it or touch it, and it's no longer in the bank account, that's when all trouble breaks out. Stop worrying when you can't see the way clearly. Worrying is our inability to trust God. We are saying God is not big enough to handle our problem. I am reminded of the story about Faith and Sight.

One day, Faith and Sight were talking; Sight said, "All you do is believe in what you cannot see. Come on, get behind me, and follow so I can show you what life is all about." Sight took Faith through the flower garden and began to name all the flowers. "That's a moonflower, that's a morning glory, and that's a passionflower over there." Then Sight took Faith through the forest and began naming all the trees. "That's an oak tree there, hickory tree over there, that's a poplar tree, and a pine tree here." They kept on walking up the road until they came to this massive rock in the road, and Sight was just bragging and said, "I can even tell you how old this rock is and how long it has been there." They continued walking until they came to this river, and Sight was looking but saw no bridge or boat. Sight stops in his tracks. Faith touched Sight on the shoulder and said, "Hey bud, keep going." Sight said, "I can't go any farther because I don't see a way to the other side."

Faith said to Sight, "You took me on a journey, bragging about the things along the way, and now here we are at the river, and you can't go any farther? Hey bud, you get behind me, and let me show you what life is all about." Faith took Sight on that same journey again. "You took me through the flower garden, and you named all the flowers, but you forgot to mention the "*Rose of Sharon*" and the "*Lily of the Valley*." Then you took me through the forest and named all the trees, but you never said anything about the "*Tree of Life*." Then you took me up the road and started bragging about the giant rock we saw; you even told me how old it was and how long it had been there. However, you never mention the "*Rock of Ages*." Now here we are at the river, and you stop in your tracks because you can't see your way clear. Just stay behind me because I will show you what life is all about; I will step out on my Lord and Savior, who is a Bridge over Troubled Water." Are you willing to walk by faith and trust God to make a way when you cannot see it?

APPLICATION

Complete these items in a journal or notebook to reflect on today's devotional.

> 1. What does walking by faith and not by sight mean to you?
> 2. Identify areas in your life where you walked by faith.

> *"It's lack of faith that makes people afraid of meeting challenges, and I believe in myself."*
> **Muhammad Ali**

STRENGTH FOR THE JOURNEY

Notes & Takeaways

In the space below, write your top three take-aways from this chapter.

DAY THIRTY-SEVEN

AN UNSHAKEABLE FAITH

"He shall be like a tree planted by the rivers of water, that brings forth its fruit in its season, whose leaf also shall not wither; and whatever he does shall prosper."
                                             Psalm 1:3 (NKJV)

A few years ago, I heard a story about a young boy who grew up and left his hometown to seek a better life. Many years later, he went back home, but nothing there was familiar. He finally remembers the big tree in the front yard because he planted it as a kid. The tree was now old and leaning forward. In the world of imagination, the tree began to talk to the young man. "Since you've been gone, a lot has happened to me. Lightening came and struck my bark and left me naked. A tornado came and left me leaning. A freeze came and took away many of my branches, and a hurricane came and shook my foundation. I am still here through all of that because when you planted me, you dug down deep and left me with strong roots. No matter what came my way, I could withstand storms because of my strong roots. That is the way it is with God. When you get connected with God, your roots become stronger and more durable to deal with the different storms of life that will come.

In Psalm 1:3, the psalmist tells us to be like a tree planted by the rivers of water. You have to develop some strong roots in the Word of God. You have to believe that God's word will get you through. You also have to develop a prayer life in the sunshine that will carry you through when the rain comes. Trust God and have faith, no matter the circumstance, because He is able. Unshakeable faith can withstand the lightening of heartaches, the tornadoes of disappointments, and the freeze of life problems. Unshakable faith can withstand the hurricane of fear. The next time your faith gets weak, remember that you have a firm root to hold onto, and "He will never forsake you."

DAY THIRTY-SEVEN

APPLICATION

Answer this question in a journal or notebook to reflect on today's devotional.

What can you do this week to strengthen your faith to handle life's challenges?

> *"United in this determination and with unshakable faith in the cause for which we fight, we will, with God's help, go forward to our greatest victory."*
> **Dwight D. Eisenhower**

STRENGTH FOR THE JOURNEY

Notes & Takeaways

In the space below, write your top three take-aways from this chapter.

DAY THIRTY-EIGHT

PRESSURE BURSTS A PIPE

"For we do not want you to be unaware, brothers, of the affliction we experienced in Asia. For we were so utterly burdened beyond our strength that we despaired of life itself. Indeed, we felt that we had received the sentence of death. But that was to make us rely not on ourselves but on God who raises the dead. He delivered us from such a deadly peril, and he will deliver us. On him, we have set our hope that he will deliver us again."

2 Corinthian 1:8-10 (ESV)

I heard the phrase "pressure bursts a pipe" from my brother Charles in high school. I played on the high school basketball team, and he always reminded me not to let the pressure get to me. He said that as long as the game is not close, it is easy for anyone to play their regular game, but most players don't want the ball when the game gets tight. They run away from it. He went on to say pressure separates the good players from the great players. That always stayed with me.

It's the same way in life; pressure is everywhere around us. There is pressure on the job to perform, pressure to meet deadlines, marriage pressure, and pressure raising your kids. A friend shared with me how he had a wonderful supervisor who would do anything for the group. However, he could not deal with pressure. He would change into a different person whenever he had deadlines to meet because he let the pressure get to him. His hands would begin to shake, he would get nervous, and he could not think clearly. He would be under so much pressure you could see it in his face. He was about to burst like my brother Charles said, "Pressure bursts a pipe." How do you survive the pressures of life and not explode?

    The Apostle Paul had a strategy for handling the pressure of life. In 2 Corinthians 1:8-10 (ESV), we see that Paul first relied on God to handle the pressure for him; second, he knew God would deliver him from the pressure of life. Finally, Paul set his hope on God. Yes, too much pressure is not good for you, but your load will get lighter when you turn it over to God.

DAY THIRTY-EIGHT

APPLICATION

I've learned that the ability to handle and thrive under pressure is a virtue of good proactive leadership. Actually, it's important to set a target and set the required pressure needed for achievement than waiting to react to the consequences of unplanned pressure, which often leads to stress.

> *"Pressure can burst a pipe, or pressure can make a diamond."*
> **— Robert Horry**

STRENGTH FOR THE JOURNEY

Notes & Takeaways

In the space below, write your top three take-aways from this chapter.

DAY THIRTY-NINE

THIS IS NOT THE FINAL DESTINATION

"We can make our plans, but the LORD determines our steps."
Proverbs 16:9 (NLT)

No matter where you find yourself in life, don't give up because this is not your final destination. It is just a layover. It's a time to regroup between where you are now and where you are trying to go. A layover is a stop between flights. You are in between flights. While you are in the layover stage, there are some things you can work on to get you ready for what God has for you. Just because things are not happening for you right now does not mean it is your final destination. Carl Brashear is an excellent example of understanding that this is not my final destination but a layover. He had to overcome many obstacles in becoming a U.S. Navy Master Diver. He was also the first amputee to be certified (or, in his case, recertified) as a Navy Diver.

On March 23, 1966, while recovering a bomb off the coast of Spain, a towing line broke, causing a pipe to strike Brashear's left leg below the knee. The leg was eventually amputated, at which time Brashear sought to rehabilitate himself and be reinstated to full active duty and diving.

The movie "Men of Honor" depicts the life of Brashear, who once said, "It's not a sin to get knocked down; it's a sin to stay down." Carl Brashear credits his faith and family for helping him get through those tough times. Like Carl Brashear, this is not your final destination but a layover. Remember, *"We can make our plans, but the LORD determines our steps."* Proverbs 16:9 (NLT). God has great things for you when it's time for you to board your next flight to your final destination. All aboard; the best is yet to come.

DAY THIRTY-NINE

APPLICATION

Complete these items in a journal or notebook to reflect on today's devotional.

1. Write down the things you can be working on while you are in the layover stage in your life.
2. How does Proverbs 16:9 speak to your current situation?

"No matter how hard the battle gets or no matter how many people don't believe in your dream, Never give up!"
Eric Thomas

STRENGTH FOR THE JOURNEY

Notes & Takeaways

In the space below, write your top three take-aways from this chapter.

DAY FORTY

GETTING THROUGH THE TURBULENCE

"Teach these new disciples to obey all the commands I have given you. And be sure of this: I am with you always, even to the end of the age."

Matthew 28:20 (NLT)

The Merriam-Webster Dictionary defines turbulent as chaotic, disordered, and disruptive. All of us know something about turbulence. This has been a turbulent week for someone; there's turbulence on the job, in the home, and in the community. Everywhere you turn, you run into turbulence. Disruption has occurred between where you are and where you are trying to go. If you are not careful, turbulence can cause you to give up.

I had forgotten a story that my nephew Adrian shared with me. He was flying from Huntsville, Alabama, to Seattle, Washington, to visit me for the summer and had a terrible flight with a lot of turbulence. He was so shaken up when he got off the plane that he said, "Uncle David, I can't fly back; you will have to get me a bus or train ticket." I asked him why. He began to tell me how the turbulence had shaken the plane so terribly that it almost turned upside down.

Adrian said right before the turbulence, the pilot had announced that they should buckle up for the rest of the flight, and the pilot said, "We will be going through some rough turbulence, but I will get you through it." In other words, the pilot had told them to trust him to get them through the turbulent times.

Who do you trust to get you through the turbulence in your life? Andrae Crouch sang a song that says, "Through it all, I have learned to trust in Jesus and depend upon His word." Indeed, no matter the turbulent, hang on to the promises in God's Word. Like Joshua encouraged the Israelites in Joshua 1:9, *"Have I not commanded you to be strong through the turbulent times for your God will be with you wherever you go."* Jesus said, *"And be sure of this: I am with you always, even to the end of the age."* Matthew 28:20 (NLT). No matter how long the turbulence in your life lasts, Jesus is with you. He is in the midst of the turbulence in your life, and He will deliver you if you trust him.

DAY FORTY

APPLICATION

Answer this question in a journal or notebook to reflect on today's devotional.

How do you find peace during the turbulence in your life?

"I think that I am a walking testimony to you can have scars. You can go through turbulent times and still have victory in your life."
Natalie Cole

STRENGTH FOR THE JOURNEY

Notes & Takeaways

In the space below, write your top three take-aways from this chapter.

DAY FORTY-ONE

WHAT IS IN YOUR RUCKSACK?

"But the fruit of the Spirit is love, joy, peace, longsuffering, kindness, goodness, faithfulness, gentleness, self-control."
Galatians 5:22–23 (NKJV)

A rucksack is a backpack that you carry on your back. For 25 years, I participated in ruck marches with soldiers at various duty stations. The ruck march tested our stamina and endurance and helped with our overall fitness. The Commander set the weight standard for the ruck. The morning before the ruck march, the Commander would have everyone weigh their ruck to ensure they had the correct number of pounds. Now and then, a few soldiers would have to add to the ruck to come up to the standard. The Commander would put out a packing list of the minimum that needed to be in our rucksacks to survive the ruck march. In the end, we were all exhausted and sweaty, and our feet hurt, but we survived.

Just like physical ruck marches, there are daily spiritual ruck marches. What is in your spiritual rucksack? What do you need in your spiritual ruck to survive the day-to-day journey? COVID-19 is causing stress, robbing people of their joy and peace of mind. If we are not careful, this pandemic will zap our strength and ruin our lives. Paul tells us what we need in our spiritual rucks to make it through these difficult days. He said we need the fruit of the Spirit. Having the fruit of the Spirit in your rucksack will give you the stamina and endurance to overcome life's struggles.

DAY FORTY-ONE

APPLICATION

Remember everyone you meet is carrying a sack of problems on their back. Be kind to them. Don't be the person that adds weight to their load. This week, reflect on Galatians 5:22, and add some fruit of the Spirit to your rucksack.

> *"Grow deep roots to harvest rich fruit! When your roots run deep, you cannot help but bear the fruit of the Spirit."*
> **Michael Beckwith**

STRENGTH FOR THE JOURNEY

Notes & Takeaways

In the space below, write your top three take-aways from this chapter.

DAY FORTY-TWO

A PASSION TO SERVE

"Their only suggestion was that we keep on helping the poor, which I have always been eager to do."

Galatians 2:10 (NIV)

The Galatians asks Paul to remember the poor and keep helping them. Paul responded that I have always helped the poor, and I am not about to stop now. Paul knew that someone had to help the less fortunate. Paul had a passion for serving, and he was a champion for the poor in the Galatians community.

My cousin Tarsha Lockhart is also a champion of the poor. Ever since she was a little child, she always has been concerned about the oppressed and those who struggled with basic necessities. When I heard she was selected to serve as the chair for the United Way Campaign at Alabama A & M University, where she is a proud alumnus. I was not surprised because she has a passion for serving. Tarsha took the United

Way Campaign at Alabama A & M to new heights under her leadership. Furthermore, Tarsha gave all the credit to her team and supporters because she is a faithful servant leader.

Passion, persistence, and patience are the secrets of Tarsha Lockhart's success. One of my success steps is to find your passion, and your work will always be enjoyable. Tarsha's passion for helping people has always been her desire, so it was easy for her to get that engine going to provide leadership to her team. Second, Tarsha is the most persistent person I know, and she will not give up until the mission is completed. Her determination to get things done is second to none. Third, Tarsha is very patient. She knows her hard work will pay off, and she consistently demonstrates patience in the face of delays.

Do you have a passion for serving? Is God calling you to serve? It could be a passion to serve in your local community or church. There are so many opportunities to serve. As the Church in Galatians said to Paul, all we ask you to do is don't forget about the poor and continuously help them. Can you step up like Paul and find your place to make a difference in people's lives.

PRAYER

God, give us the passion for serving those who are less fortunate and need our help in meeting the basic necessity of life. God, please give us the strength and courage to help us fight for better health care, education, and financial stability for the poor, for in so doing, we are serving you.

APPLICATION

Answer this question in a journal or notebook to reflect on today's devotional.

Where can you volunteer your resources this month to make a difference in people's lives? The resources may include time, talent, or monetary sacrifice.

> *"Nothing great in the world has ever been accomplished without passion."*
> **Georg Wilhelm Friedrich Hegel**

STRENGTH FOR THE JOURNEY

Notes & Takeaways

In the space below, write your top three take-aways from this chapter.

DAY FORTY-THREE

END OF THE YEAR INVENTORY

"Brethren, I do not count myself to have apprehended; but one thing I do, forgetting those things which are behind and reaching forward to those things which are ahead."

Philippians 3:13 (NKJV)

In 2017, I was the Garrison Chaplain at Fort Bragg, NC. Sergeant (SGT) Chava Jones, who was Private First Class (PFC) Chava Jones at the time, was my supply Non-Commissioned Officer (NCO). Usually, an NCO holds that job, but I put SGT Jones in that position. She did an excellent job running the supply room for soldiers, airmen on the installation. What impressed me the most about SGT Jones was how she executed the end-of-the-year inventory. She was swamped at the end of the fiscal year, trying to account for the supplies during inventory. This was a very tedious and lengthy process. However, SGT Jones had accounted for all of our property at the end of the inventory. Because she did such a great job on the inventory, we could turn in supplies that the Religious Support Teams (RST) were not using and order more supplies to distribute to the RSTs. We made adjustments for the coming year through Chava's leadership and provided religious support to Fort Bragg RSTs.

Like the physical end-of-the-year inventory, we need to take a spiritual end-of-the-year inventory and see what adjustments are needed, what needs to be left in the old year, and what we need to carry over into the new year. Paul is taking inventory of his life in Philippians 3:13.

Three points Paul wants to get across concerning our end-of-the-year inventories:

> **The Past** "Forgetting those things which are behind" - The past may include past hurts, failures, setbacks, and disappointments. You have to let go of the past to embrace the future. You may have to forgive and forget to grasp a new and better chapter in your life.
>
> **The Present** The present may include things hindering you from working toward a better tomorrow, settling for a comfort zone far below your potential.
>
> **The Future** "Reaching forward to those things which are ahead" - Often, the things ahead call for focus and hard work. It may also require us to shift focus to achieve a better tomorrow.

DAY FORTY-THREE

Destiny is a matter of choice and should not be left to chance; God's divine leading every step of the way will sail you through smoothly to a glorious and desirable destiny that glorifies Him.

APPLICATION

Take an end-of-the-year inventory of your spiritual life, measure your progress, and make the necessary adjustments to walk into a better year.

> *"Don't kid yourself. Be honest with yourself. Take your own inventory."*
>
> **Jack Canfield**

STRENGTH FOR THE JOURNEY

Notes & Takeaways

In the space below, write your top three take-aways from this chapter.

DAY FORTY-FOUR

THE GOD OF A SECOND CHANCE

"Because of the Lord's great love we are not consumed, for his compassions never fail. They are new every morning; great is your faithfulness."

Lamentations 3:22-23 (NIV)

I will never forget the summer of 1981; I was injured prone, had a nagging injury I could not shake, and missed quite a few games at Snead State Junior College. After the season, I was unsure if I would get a second chance to play college basketball. I worked so hard the summer of 1982, hoping I would get a second chance with a program that needed a point guard. I felt I had recovered, and I was healthy for the first time in over a year. That summer, I was named the Most Valuable Player in the Huntsville Basketball City League. I wanted to continue playing college basketball in my heart, but it seemed like that opportunity was over. I had concluded that I would not get a second chance in a good program. I was in the kitchen telling my mom I would not try to play basketball anymore at the collegiate level. I remember these words from my mother, "If it's God's will, you will get a second chance."

I was in my room the next day, and the phone rang. My mother said it was Coach Randy Dunn, Assistant Basketball Coach from North Georgia College. He told me, "David, we need a point guard. Do you want to come here and play?" I knew he never saw me play, but he said a few coaches told him that I was a good point guard and could run a team.

Coach Dunn drove over to Sparkman High School in Toney, Alabama, and Coach Stanley Stafford opened the gym. Coach Dunn had me shoot around and do some drills. He offered me a scholarship on the spot and said if I came to North Georgia College, we would go to the National Championship. We went two years in a row, and after my last year, he was instrumental in getting me my first job. We developed a bond that went far beyond coach and player. Not only was he a great coach, teacher, and mentor in my life, he was my friend and an all-around great person. We bonded instantly. You never know who God is sending in your life to give you a second chance. We have to be ready and available when our second chances in life come. We serve a God of a second chance; He doesn't give up on us if we don't get it right the first time around.

"Because of the Lord's great love we are not consumed, for his compassions never fail. They are new every morning; great is your faithfulness."

DAY FORTY-FOUR

Lamentations 3:22-23 (NIV). The Prophet Jeremiah, in this chapter, refers to his personal experience under affliction as an example of how the people of Judah should behave under their afflictions to have hope of restoration. The God we serve is filled with great love and compassion that never fails and second chances that never cease.

Like myself, you may find yourself injury-prone from hurtful situations in life, and it appears opportunities in life are over. Let me be that voice of encouragement like my mom was years ago. God's wish for us is summed up in 3 John 2 (KJV), *"Beloved, I wish above all things that thou mayest prosper and be in health, even as thy soul prospereth."* Because of God's great love and compassion, his second chances for us are endless.

APPLICATION

This week as we look back over our life, taking note of the numerous second chances God has given us, let us be compassionate and pay forward second chances to others along our journey.

> *"If somebody is gracious enough to give me a second chance, I won't need a third."*
>
> **Pete Rose**

DAY FORTY-FIVE

COMBATTING SUICIDE IDEATION

"Behold, I am the LORD, the God of all flesh. Is there anything too hard for Me?"

Jeremiah 32:27 (NKJV)

Have you ever had suicidal thoughts? Have you ever been in a place you could not get out of, and you thought you would be better off gone? Hold on, please! It can get wearisome when you have nowhere to go back, yet the path ahead is dark. You can't see where to move forward to either, and in other words, you are stuck in a dark place in life's journey. You can't move back or forward. The devil can use this to harbor suicidal thoughts.

This week, I talked with my battle buddy John Morris about a few recent suicides. He said a person could have everything money could buy, but money can't buy happiness. John stated that we often overlook the people who are always giving and seen like they have their lives together. However, those are the ones we need to check on a little more. It doesn't hurt to ask someone how they are really doing. For example, by asking, "Is there anything I can do to help you today," you might make a difference. Remember to tell people, "If you need someone to talk to, I am here for you."

Though depression plays a role in most suicides, the sense of hopelessness and helplessness that spurs on suicide can have other origins. Remember, behind every physical happening is a spiritual cause. We live in two worlds – the physical and spiritual world. Events first happen in the spiritual realm, and if not stopped through prayers, they manifest in the physical world. Some people under great stress move quickly toward suicide with little or no warning.

People considering suicide often display one or more of the following moods: depression, anxiety, loss of interest, irritability, humiliation/shame, agitation/anger, grief, sexual abuse, financial problems, a relationship breakup, or substance abuse. No one really wants to die; they just want the pain to stop. I always heard that suicide is a permanent solution to a temporary problem. So how do we help people overcome this temporary problem and have the will to live through this temporary problem?

As a Christian, you have no right to take away your life. 1 Corinthians 6:19-20 explains that you are not your own; you were bought at a price. Remember Jeremiah 29:11, knowing that ultimately God will come forth to your rescue. It may take a while, but hang on to Him regardless of any predicament. *"'For I know the plans I have for you,' declares the Lord, 'plans to prosper you and not to harm you, plans to give you hope and a future.'"* Jeremiah 29:11 (NIV). Remember, God is unlimited. *"Behold, I am the LORD, the God of all flesh. Is there anything too hard for Me?"* (Jeremiah 32:27 (NKJV).

PRAYER

Holy God,
Working with people at risk of suicide can be very demanding. Please help us alleviate our fears, self-doubt, and misappropriate attitudes so we can be ready and able to help preserve the lives of our friends, loved ones, and whoever we come in contact with. Amen.

APPLICATION

Answer this question in your journal or notebook.

What is your strategy to help people who have suicidal ideation?

> *"Never, never, never give up."*
> **Winston Churchill**

Notes & Takeaways

In the space below, write your top three take-aways from this chapter.

DAY FORTY-SIX

HOW HIGH DO YOU ASPIRE TO GO?

"Follow my example, as I follow the example of Christ."

1 Corinthians 11:1 (NIV)

"Join together in following my example, brothers and sisters, and just as you have us as a model, keep your eyes on those who live as we do."

Philippians 3:17 (NIV)

A.A. Hedge says that "No man can ever rise above that at which he aims." What targets in life are you aiming to hit? How high do you want to go? Do you have a burning desire to aspire for the extra-ordinary? Second Lieutenant Francisco Pena was Specialist (SPC) Francisco Pena in 2017 when he was on my Religious Support Staff at Fort Bragg. I have never met an individual who was so driven. I remember during a one-on-one session, I asked SPC Pena' what are you passionate about, and what do you aspire to do in life? He said Chaplain Lockhart, I want to be a Chaplain because I have a servant heart. I said Specialist Pena you have qualities every great Chaplain should have; the heart, the attitude and compassion. You can go as high as you aspire to go.

Lieutenant Pena recently contacted me, sharing some heartfelt words every servant leader can appreciate. He said, "Sir believe me, you inspired me to become a Chaplain. Thank you for everything. You can say the same that Paul said, in I Corinthians 11:1 and Philippians 3:17. The Apostle Paul expressed in I Corinthians 11:1 that we should carefully follow the directions and imitate him as he follows Christ the perfect example. Paul continues to express the importance of following a godly example in Philippians 3:17, where he admonishes us to follow him as he follows Christ, and those who exemplify the characteristics of Christ; in that you will find the example to follow.

Lieutenant Pena continued to emphasize that the godly example that I displayed before him daily was the reason He followed his passion to become an Army Chaplain. Whereas it's quite difficult for me to accept accolades about something I am passionate about doing, coaching, teaching, and mentoring are just who I am. I accepted Lieutenant Pena's compliments with sincere humility. At the time of publishing, Lieutenant Pena is preparing for graduation from the Chaplain Officer Basic Course on April 21, 2022 and graduation from seminary at the end of this year. Lieutenant Pena words reminded me of Matthew 5:16, *"Let your light so shine before men, that they see your good works and glorify God which is in Heaven."* Never minimize your assignments from God, you never know whose life you may impact God's glory.

APPLICATION

Always live a life that exemplifies the characteristics of Christ to the point others may see your passion for Christ, perhaps even follow in your footsteps, but ultimately follow Christ the perfect example.

> *"Desire, burning desire, is basic to achieving anything beyond the ordinary."*
> **Joseph B. Wirthlin**

DAY FORTY-SEVEN

WORDS MATTER

"Gentle words are a tree of life; a deceitful tongue crushes the spirit."

Proverbs 15:4 (NLT)

Minister and Life Coach Charlesetta Kelly Brinson is a licensed minister of the Gospel at Hope Community and the founder and CEO of Gen3 Life Coach and Consulting LLC. She wrote a self-empowerment book titled Path To Purpose, illustrating the importance of the words we speak to others and ourselves. Our words matter. Learn the power of your words and how they can illuminate your path to purpose and empower others when appropriately used. It is vital to use our words; they can be enriching or discouraging. Words are an essential part of our existence. On average, most people say at least 10,000 words per day. While we often emphasize carefully selecting the words we say to others, we are not often considerate enough of the words we say to ourselves. In her book, she demonstrates the power of words through her own 52 Words and Life Application Short Stories. I agree that words are important. They can discourage us or encourage us; they can give us hope or cause us to give up on our dreams. According to the Bible, we need to choose our words carefully.

There is power in words, and as anointed children of God, we should use our words to build. Our words should be used to decree what is progressive to the kingdom, and it will be established (Job 22:28).

Proverbs 16:24 (NLT) says, *"Kind words are like honey-sweet to the soul and healthy for the body."* Kind words also cheer the heart and our strides; they restore vigor to the depressed. Wisdom must guide your speech and the tone used to minister grace to the hearers.

Proverbs 18:4 (NLT), *"Wise words are like deep waters; wisdom flows from the wise like a bubbling brook."* As you can see through Path To Purpose and the wisdom from the Bible, choosing and using our words wisely impacts others and ourselves.

APPLICATION

Make a mental or actual note of the words you speak to yourself and others this week, then evaluate if they were encouraging or discouraging. Since we speak 10,000 words daily, let them be positive. Words matter.

> "Words are powerful. They can make or break a person. Whispering words of wisdom can empower, encourage, uplift and help move someone forward. Choose KIND words to heal one's spirit."
>
> **Ritu Ghatourey**

STRENGTH FOR THE JOURNEY

Notes & Takeaways

In the space below, write your top three take-aways from this chapter.

DAY FORTY-EIGHT

ARE YOU PREPARED TO WIN?

"Do you not know that those who run in a race all run, but one receives the prize? Run in such a way that you may obtain it."
1 Corinthians 9:24 (NKJV)

Coach Antonio Henderson, my former Chaplain Assistant, is an Assistant Football Coach at Lakeside High School in Augusta, Georgia. He shared some insight with me a few weeks ago on preparing for a football game. Coach Henderson is very passionate about football and said he and the other coaches watch films all week to understand what they will be up against in the coming week. The film lets them know the possible strategies of the opposing players that give them the most trouble. The film provides insight into putting players in a position to win the game strategically. How often do we study films on our spiritual journey? The Bible says, *"The thief does not come except to steal, and to kill, and to destroy."* John 10:10 (NKJV). We need to study the films (scriptures) to recognize the devil's schemes and understand who we are up against and how to counter his moves.

Coach Henderson also shared the importance of studying the playbook to see what plays are in it and give his team the advantages against the team they will be facing that week. They look for weaknesses that they can exploit. They may even put in new plays on offense and defense to give them an advantage. Have you ever noticed we have a sixty-six-volume playbook called the Bible? Do we look into the playbook daily to see how we can win when Satan tries to knock us down and knock us out from following our faith? Do we develop new offenses and defenses to prevail against the enemy's attacks? *"All Scripture is God-breathed and is useful for teaching, rebuking, correcting and training in righteousness, so that the servant of God may be thoroughly equipped for every good work."* 2 Timothy 3:16-17 (NIV).

Coach Henderson and the other coaches executed a walk-through of what they saw on film and added to the playbook. Afterward, they put the team through a walk-through so their players would know how to handle any of the schemes of the opposing team. This would also allow them to take advantage of the opposing team's weakness. Preparation may not guarantee a win, but it sure puts you in position for one. In our spiritual walk, we constantly do walk-

DAY FORTY-EIGHT

throughs to keep us grounded in the Word and the ability to see the light on the path we are walking. *His Word is a lamp for my feet, a light on my path.* (Psalm 119:105).

The exciting truth is that there is a word for any challenge we encounter in this life; however, you need to have the scripture in your spirit. When bombarded by a challenge, Holy Spirit simply reminds you of scriptures already in your spirit. This calls for a need to be fully grounded in the Word of God. The scripture is a sword you use to face the enemy when attacked. Can you imagine a soldier who, when attacked, is found armless and has to look back first to pick his arms for defense? The enemy would wipe him off in the process of him turning around to look for his armory. Likewise, as Christians, we should be ready at all times with our sword of the Spirit, which is the Word of God. For every challenge, you answer with the relevant phrase as Jesus did. Tell the circumstance, "It is written;" say to the devil, "It is written." You can't do so if you don't spend time studying your playbook (Bible). Meditate on the Word and let it sink deep in your spirit as you prepare to win on this spiritual journey.

Coach Henderson closes with these words: *"We have to keep the kids focused and motivated to win."* Likewise, we must stay focused on the prize on our spiritual journey and stay motivated to win the race. *"Do you not know that those who run in a race all run, but one receives the prize? Run in such a way that you may obtain it."* 1 Corinthians 9:24 (NKJV).

APPLICATION

Whatever we need to prepare for daily and excel at, may we stay focused and determined to win. I pray for foresight and sharpness of mind for each of us during our preparation time.

> *"It's not the will to win that matters- everyone has that. It's the will to prepare to win that matters."*
>
> **Paul "Bear" Bryant**

DAY FORTY-NINE

BE THANKFUL

"In everything give thanks; for this is the will of God in Christ Jesus for you."

1 Thessalonica 5:18 (NKJV)

No matter our situation, we can be thankful for what God has done for us and for what God promises to do for us. Thanksgiving Day is a time to reflect and be grateful for all God has given us. Most of us have not learned to express our gratitude when times are hard. In September of 2021, one of my best friends from college, Norris Ratliff, was in a severe car accident. He described to me what had happened. He said David; I was driving up the interstate in Georgia on a beautiful day. I was on a mission for my job to complete a task. I noticed the traffic slowed down and came to a complete stop. The SUV behind me was not paying attention and hit me at high speed, and I was sandwiched between two cars. The ambulance came and took me to the emergency room, and then it was there I realized I could not walk.

Norris left leg was broken in two places. So Norris is in the hospital with a broken tibia-fibula, severe shoulder pain, and a swollen right hand and right leg. The police said he was fortunate to survive this crash. Then on top of all of this, the doctor came in and said that to save Norris' leg, they would have to do emergency surgery in two days. They put a plate and screws in his leg. I said Norris, I am so sorry this happened to such a wonderful person like you. Before I could get another sentence out, Norris said, David, don't feel sorry for me. I am so thankful to be alive, and God brought me through this for a reason. Norris has faith in God that in the coming months, he will walk again. Instead of having a self-pity party, Norris thanked God for bringing him through. It is easy to thank God when everything is going well, but Norris thanks him "despite going through a hard time."

The Bible says, *"In everything give thanks; for this is the will of God in Christ Jesus for you."* (1 Thessalonica 5:18 (NKJV). The Apostle Paul gives us words to live by; he wants us to express joy in everything, never stop praying, and give thanks in everything. It should become routine to thank God in every situation you find yourself in.

Paul wants us to grasp that God is in control no matter what we are going through. We are not thankful for the hard days, however we are thankful because God brings us through the hard times. "God promises never to leave us or forsake us. "At the grave of Lazarus. Jesus said, father, I thank you for always hearing me (John 11:41); what a way to start a prayer in the face of a predicament! Jesus understood the reason for Thanksgiving! Thanksgiving draws God's attention and unleashes his divine power.

APPLICATION

This week, make a list of all the things you are thankful for. Johnson Oatman's (1897) song reminds us to *"Count your blessings and see what God has done for you; you will be surprised at what God has done."*

> *"Never let the things you want make you forget the things you have."*
> **Anonymous**

STRENGTH FOR THE JOURNEY

Notes & Takeaways

In the space below, write your top three take-aways from this chapter.

DAY FIFTY

FREEDOM IS NEVER FREE

"Trust in the LORD with all your heart, and lean not on your own understanding; in all your ways acknowledge Him, and He shall direct your paths."
Proverbs 3:5-6 (NKJV)

I befriended Chaplain (COL-Ret) John Morris in 1995 while we both served as chaplains in the 3rd Infantry, 2nd Brigade at Fort Stewart, Georgia. Our friendship has grown stronger each year, and we are still best friends. I also served with John in 2009 in Iraq. During this time, John was responsible for coordinating religious support for all Soldiers, Sailors, Airmen, and Marines in Iraq in Regional Command South (RC-S) in Basra, Iraq. He provided exceptional technical and tactical advice to his Commander to enable the proficient planning and provision of religious support for all units in the command.

Chaplain Morris not only contributed to the overall welfare of his team as the Command Chaplain, but he was also responsible for religious support personnel throughout the entire RC-S. His team provided uninterrupted religious support activities both in preparation for and in the execution of combat operations. John traveled at extreme personal risk, coming under small arms fire and the risk of rocket-propelled grenades, improvised explosive devices, and indirect fire from mortar and rocket attacks. One particular day, he showed up for a meeting at Camp Victory in Iraq, where I worked, and he looked so tired and worn out. I could tell he had gone days without sleep. I said, "John, you need to rest," and he said, "I can't until every service member has had an opportunity to attend religious service according to their faith."

John always put the mission first, which led to him being inducted into the Minnesota Military Hall of Fame this year. I asked John a few months ago what it was that sustained him during those challenging times in combat and what scripture he leaned on. He said, "My faith in God got me through, and my favorite scripture is Proverbs 3:5-6. *"Trust in the LORD with all your heart, And lean not on your own understanding; In all your ways acknowledge Him, And He shall direct your paths."*Proverbs 3:5-6 (NKJV). I can see why CH Morris picked this verse because when we trust in the Lord with all our heart, we can keep going; it is because we gave our hearts to God. When we lean not to our own understanding, we're saying, "Lord, I surrender all to

DAY FIFTY

you because you know what is best for me." When we acknowledge Him, we tell God, "You are in control of my life, and I will follow wherever you lead me." When we let God direct our path, He gives us the strength not to be weary, as promised in Isaiah 40:31. Indeed, when we trust in the Lord with all our hearts, we learn to wait on Him because we know He is too faithful to fail. Yes, He will usher us to awesome destinies. Beloved, wait on God. Today, I salute Chaplain (COL Retired) John Morris for going beyond the call of duty in serving our country during Operation Iraqi Freedom. I pray God blesses every veteran in our nation, and may they feel appreciated by the citizens of this great nation. Let every veteran feel the deep and enduring gratitude of our country.

APPLICATION

President John F. Kennedy said, "As we express our gratitude, we must never forget that the highest appreciation is not to utter words but to live by them." Add some action to the words we utter to a veteran this week. Words Matter!

> "No one had served the country better than our greatest Veterans! They sacrificed their lives for the sake of many and for the freedom of our country. With great gratitude, we salute you for the honor and freedom you brought to this country!"
>
> **Unknown**

DAY FIFTY-ONE

NEVER GIVE UP ON YOUR DREAMS

"With God all things are possible."
Matthew 19:26 (NIV)

Eddie Harris Jr., a motivational speaker, said, "It takes a dream to get started, desire to keep going, and determination to finish." When I think about this quote, Staff Sergeant Sabrina Mireles, who was then Specialist Sabrina Mireles, exemplifies Eddie Harris's quote to the fullness. In 2018, Sabrina was one of my high-speed Chaplain Assistants in the 108th Brigade in San Antonio, TX. Her story is fascinating and will motivate you not to give up on your dreams. Her dream was to get her bachelor's degree, but no one in her family had been to college. None of her friends had attended either, and no one at her high school had encouraged her to attend college. So she felt like she was doing it alone. However, she was willing to keep going and stay on course. I asked Sabrina what kept her going and gave her the determination to finish. She gave all credit to God and shared with me that, *"With God all things are possible."* Matthew 19:26 (KJV) is the scripture she leans on many times to overcome her obstacles and challenges. She thanked God for never taking His hands off of her. Sabrina acknowledged God for letting her conquer far beyond what anyone could have thought possible. She thanked her mother for being the backbone and number one supporter in her life. Sabrina says that if you saw her in high school, you wouldn't have thought she would have graduated with a bachelor's and masters' degree while serving her country on active duty and still going to school for her Ph.D. She gave God all the praise and glory for taking her from the dirt roads in Burton, South Carolina and transforming her into a success story.

What an amazing testimony from a remarkable young lady, and I just pulled a few excerpts from her story. Sabrina also dreams of becoming an officer in the United States Army in the near future. I hope she puts her story in a book one day because she surely has a story to tell. When we learn how to trust and lean on God, we can conquer our dreams. Yes, there will be challenges and obstacles, but "With God, all things are possible." Never allow anyone to stop you from dreaming because your dreams are possible.

That great poet Langston Hughes was correct when he penned the poem: "Hold fast to dreams, For if dreams die, Life is a broken-winged bird, That cannot fly. Hold fast to dreams, For when dreams go, Life is a barren field, Frozen with snow." Don't let anyone take your dreams away. The dream may not be easy, but it is possible because, "With God, all things are possible."

APPLICATION

Complete these items in a journal or notebook to reflect on today's devotional.

    1. This week, meditate on Matthew 19:26.
    2. Write down what this scripture is saying to you each day in a journal.

> *"It takes a dream to get started, desire to keep going, and determination to finish."*
> **Eddie Harris Jr.**

STRENGTH FOR THE JOURNEY

Notes & Takeaways

In the space below, write your top three take-aways from this chapter.

DAY FIFTY-TWO

MORE BLESSED TO GIVE THAN RECEIVE

"'It is more blessed to give than to receive.'"

Acts 20:35 (NLT)

Acts 20:35 talks of being a vessel through which many receive their blessing. When God sees the state of your heart and willingness to bless others, he will utilize you as a conduit to bless others. We are just vessels; wealth is not for pride or showing off but to sustainably bless and transform humanity for the glory of God as God leads us. We celebrate Christmas because God gave (John 3:16), and he gave because he loved the world. You can give without loving, but you can't love and not give, however small the giving may be.

While there are so many beautiful Christmas stories, one of my favorites is about a boy named William Spurling. William was big for his age and struggled academically as well as socially. However, he was a good kid and well-liked by his seventh-grade classmates.

For the Christmas school play about the birth of Jesus, William dreamed of being a shepherd. Sadly, the teacher said he was too big and better suited to play the grumpy old innkeeper. On the night of the play, during the part when Mary and Joseph come to the door, asking for a place to sleep, William, in a gruff voice, said, "There is no room in the inn."

Joseph asked again, and instead of repeating the scripted response, William forgot his line. There was an uncomfortable pause. The kind of pause that embarrasses everyone on stage, as well as the audience. Then, from behind the curtain, William's teacher whispered the line, "We have no room at the inn, now away with you!" Dutifully, he repeated the line. Dejected, Mary and Joseph turned to walk away.

Being the good kid he was, William felt his heart begin to break because of his words of rejection. He yelled out, "Wait a minute! Come back! You can have my room, and I will sleep in the shed!"

Consider this, instead of the play being ruined, William unwittingly displayed the true meaning of Christmas. It is more blessed to give than to receive. Giving is a Godly principle that every Christian should practice. God the Father is the greatest giver. He exemplified it by giving his only begotten son (John 3:16); God has a mighty harvest of souls worshipping

DAY FIFTY-TWO

him eternally from this giving. The Bible says God loves a cheerful giver (2 Cor 9: 6-8), so never give while murmuring or complaining. You will only delay or possibly abort your harvest.

Furthermore, consider the 3S's before giving: the seed, soil, and season. The seed quality speaks of the state of your heart, motive, sanctity, and level of sacrifice, not the amount of the seed sown (this varies with how much one is blessed). The soil speaks of the fire on the altar you are sowing into; any altar or kingdom cause recognized by Heaven will attract a reward. The season speaks of timing; know when to plant your seed and exercise patience as it grows. You need to water your seed/plants as they grow by being positive, meditating on the Word, and focusing on kingdom service.

STRENGTH FOR THE JOURNEY

APPLICATION

Complete these items in a journal or notebook to reflect on today's devotional.

How can you apply Acts 20:35 in this season?

> *"If it is more blessed to give than to receive, then most of us are content to let the other fellow have the greater blessing."*
> **— Shailer Mathews**

DAY FIFTY-THREE

STAYING ON COURSE

"Commit to the Lord whatever you do, and he will establish your plans."

Proverbs 16:3 (NIV)

In 2009, in Iraq, I met Chief Master Sergeant (CMSgt) Theresa Grolla, then Master Sergeant Grolla. She always had a passion for serving Christ and a passion for fitness. She was an usher for the worship service that I supervised. I noticed she was always one of the first ushers to arrive at the service. I remember these words: "Chaplain, anything you need for the service, please let me know." CMS Grolla was always ready and available to help out in the worship service. Even with her full-time job in the Air Force and serving in a combat environment, she also had a passion for training for fitness competitions. Her process for attacking anything in life is her three Ds (principles), which has kept her on course: "Dedicate yourself to the job," "Desire to do it," and

"Determination to get the job done." Chief Master Sergeant (CMSgt) Grolla applied her three Ds to place in several fitness competitions and credits her three Ds to her successful career in the Air Force. However, sad to say, many of us got off course and missed the mark. According to the Merriam-Webster dictionary, staying on course means to continue with a process, effort, even though it is difficult. Sometimes, in life, we lose focus and get off course. There's a story told about a bloodhound in England that started a hunt by chasing a large buck. A fox crossed his path during the chase, so he began to chase the fox. A rabbit crossed his hunting path, so he began to go after the rabbit. After chasing the rabbit for a while, a tiny field mouse crossed his path. He chased the mouse to the corner of a farmer's barn. The bloodhound, which began the hunt chasing a prized deer, wound up barking at a tiny mouse. Have you ever gotten off of your spiritual course and needed a reboot? If so, CMSgt Grolla's three D principles can get you back on the right course.

Dedication – *"Commit to the Lord whatever you do, and he will establish your plans."* Proverbs 16:3 (NIV)
Dedicate yourself to whatever task God has called you to do, and He will bring it to pass.

Desire – *"But seek first the kingdom of God and His righteousness, and all these things shall be added to you."* Matthew 6:33 (NKJV)
When you desire to put God first, He will give you

everything you need. Sometimes, we are misled by what we want, but God knows best what we need. He will put it in our lives as we focus on serving Him.

Determination – *"Don't you realize that in a race everyone runs, but only one person gets the prize? So run to win! All athletes are disciplined in their training."* 1 Corinthians 9:24-25 (NLT)

Above all, it's important to establish the will of God for one's life and focus on pursuing it.

APPLICATION

Complete these items in a journal or notebook to reflect on today's devotional.

1. Are you staying on the course God has for you, or do you need to get back on track?
2. This week, meditate on Matthew 19:26 and write down in a journal daily what this scripture is saying to you.

The three D principles to stay on course of your goal: "Dedicate yourself to the job," "Desire to do it," and "Determination to get the job done."
Chief Master Sergeant Theresa Grolla

STRENGTH FOR THE JOURNEY

Notes & Takeaways

In the space below, write your top three take-aways from this chapter.

DAY FIFTY-FOUR

HAVING A SERVANT'S HEART

"For even the Son of Man came not to be served but to serve, and to give his life as a ransom for many."
Mark 10:45 (ESV)

When the Son of Man is Lord of our lives, it can be seen in how we serve others. We demonstrate our love for God by serving all people with dignity and respect.

A servant's heart is when we give of ourselves and do not expect anything in return. We show a servant's heart when we give our time, love, and money without expecting recognition. When I think of a servant's heart, I need to look no further than my cousin Pastor Anthony Stewart, who pastored for over forty years. I never met anyone in any field of work who comes close to exemplifying a servant's heart more than Anthony. Pastor Stewart never asked anyone to do what he was not willing to do. He always met the needs of his parishioners, always putting them first. Whatever needed to be done in the church, he was always out front serving with the people.

Pastor Stewart must have been aware of the scriptures. According to Mathew 10:42, there is a sure reward for kingdom service as small as a glass of cold water given in the name of the Lord. Moreover, Exodus 23:25-26 further promises health and longevity as part of the rewards for kingdom service. The true rewarder for kingdom service is Jehovah, God Himself! Keep on serving wholeheartedly, not as men and women pleasers (Ephesians 6:7) but as those serving the Lord wholeheartedly, and you will not lose your reward (Mathew 10:42).

Pastor Stewart always cared about his parishioners and shared in their problems by being there for them. Pastor Stewart put me in the mind of Nehemiah. Nehemiah was not the kind of leader who liked to be in the limelight or strove to take credit for all important things. Likewise, Pastor Stewart always credited his parishioners when they accomplished any goals or received any achievements.

Do you have a servant's heart? Whose basic needs are you going to meet this year? The basic needs of humans are food, shelter, and safety. When these needs are obtained, humans reach for something higher: love and compassion. Will you demonstrate a true servant heart and meet the needs of someone the world has given up on? When we serve humankind, we serve God.

> "For I was hungry and you gave Me food; I was thirsty and you gave Me drink; I was a stranger and you took Me in; I was naked, and you clothed Me; I was sick and you visited Me; I was in prison and you came to Me."
>
> Matthew 25:35-36 (NKJV)

APPLICATION

Complete these items in a journal or notebook to reflect on today's devotional.

1. What does the phrase "not to be served, but to serve" mean to you? What is holding you back from having a servant's heart?

2. In what ways are you involved in serving God with your energy within your local community? Get involved in your community, serve God with your energy, and watch God reward you.

> "I shall pass through this world but once. Any good therefore that I can do, or any kindness that I can show to any human being, let me do it now. Let me not defer or neglect it, for I shall not pass this way again."
>
> **Henry Drummond**

STRENGTH FOR THE JOURNEY

Notes & Takeaways

In the space below, write your top three take-aways from this chapter.

DAY FIFTY-FIVE

HIS ROD AND STAFF COMFORT ME

"Yea though I walk through the valley of the shadow of death, I will fear no evil; For you are with me; Your rod and Your staff, they comfort me."

Psalm 23:4 (NKJV)

Retired Army Chaplain Archie Simmons, a good friend for over twenty-five years, tells how he survived a heart attack during his deployment to Djibouti on the Horn of Africa. Archie was under incredible stress from being overtasked and overworked. One day he had pains in his chest, and being a good soldier, he tried to push through. The pains became unbearable. Archie was medevacked to the hospital in Landstuhl, Germany, and the diagnosis was a severe heart attack. He was in intensive care for seven days. His account of how he survived is fascinating, but the most inspiring part is how he managed to keep himself going when all hope seemed lost. Chaplain Simmons said he kept encouraging himself in the Lord, remembering King David encouraged himself in the Lord. (I Samuel 30:6). Archie said he could not give up because of his family, and he knew in his heart that God wasn't through with him yet. He said God gave him the fortitude he needed to keep going, even when the situation seemed hopeless and there was no end in sight. I asked Chaplain Simmons what got him through.

He said it was Psalm 23:4 (NKJV), *"Yea though I walk through the valley of the shadow of death, I will fear no evil; For you are with me; Your rod and Your staff, they comfort me."* He kept meditating on that scripture, and after a few days, a calmness came over his body, and the pains went away. The doctors said we don't know what just happened, but all your vital signs have gone back to normal. Archie testified that God's "rod and staff" comforted him.

I don't know what you are going through this week, but God is with you. His "rod and staff" will comfort you. Some of you are going through things you never dreamed of. You are trying to figure out how to get out from underneath the heaviness that has become so unbearable. I want to encourage you to turn it over to the Lord, and His rod and staff will comfort you. His "rod and staff" will pull you out of the miry clay and plant your feet on the rock to stay.

DAY FIFTY-FIVE

APPLICATION

Answer these questions in a journal or notebook to reflect on today's devotional.

1. Have you ever felt helpless and powerless to fix a situation?
2. How did trusting the Lord as your rod and staff deliver you?

"All our infirmities, whatever they are, are just opportunities for God to display his gracious work in us."

C.H. Spurgeon

STRENGTH FOR THE JOURNEY

Notes & Takeaways

In the space below, write your top three take-aways from this chapter.

DAY FIFTY-SIX

WHAT TIME IS IT?

"Create in me a clean heart, O God, and put a new and right spirit within me."

Psalms 51:10 (NRSV)

Not long after people began to take Covid 19 shots, they came out with a booster shot. Different organizations were advertising 'we have the booster here'. Come and get your COVID booster, and there is no long line. We can get you in and out quickly. The booster shot is supposed to give your immune system a boost and strengthen your immune system from COVID. I heard one person say 'if it had not been for the booster, he would not have survived COVID'. The experts say we need to get the booster shot, and there may even be another booster soon. Maybe the COVID booster will become like the flu shot; where you get it every year.

However, I wonder today how many of us need a spiritual booster to renew us and get us to focus on our spiritual journey. If you feel spiritual drain and spiritual bankruptcy, God is ready to give you a spiritual booster. In Psalms 51:10 New Revised Standard Version (NRSV), the Bible says, "Create in me a clean heart, O God, and put a new and right spirit within me. David had sinned against the Lord for his own self-centered gain and to please his own inward lusts. Because of his sin, David's wonderful communion with God had been broken. David's joy in the Lord had been lost, and his soul was totally convicted. David realized he could not go on like this, and he knew for him to restore his relationship with God; it was time for a spiritual booster shot, which is why he uttered Psalms 51:10. David knew what time it was?

Do you know what time it is for you today? Do you need divine forgiveness? Do you need your soul to be revived, does your heart need to be restored; then it's time for you to get a spiritual booster shot! Just repeat what David said in Psalms 51:10, and God will give you a spiritual booster and restore your passion and love to serve again.

There are times you have to arise and say to yourself like the Lord said to the people at Horeb in Deuteronomy 1:6 "You have stayed long enough at this mountain." Yes; you may have stayed long enough at a given spiritual level of none or little growth; spiritually stagnant at a level of prayerlessness; sluggishness to your spiritual calling or assignment; the work of the ministry. It's time to take your spiritual booster and arise for you have stayed long enough in that mountain; resume your journey of spiritual growth!

PRAYER

Oh God, create in each of us a clean heart and renew the right spirit within us. God, we know it's time for a spiritual booster so we can serve and worship you with passion.

APPLICATION

Answer these questions in a journal or notebook to reflect on today's devotional.

1. How do you interpret Psalms 51:10?
2. Have you ever needed a spiritual booster to refocus your spiritual journey?
3. How is your spiritual growth? How are you progressing with your divine assignment?

You might be serving but behind schedule; arise!

"When God forgives, He at once restores."
Theodore Eppmility

STRENGTH FOR THE JOURNEY

Notes & Takeaways

In the space below, write your top three take-aways from this chapter.

DAY FIFTY-SEVEN

DO GOOD TOWARD ALL

"Therefore, as we have opportunity, let us do good to all people."

Galatians 6:10 (NIV)

When I was a teenager, I used to see kindness expressed throughout my community and read about it in other communities, but kindness is becoming obsolete these days. Most communities care less about others. We have become so selfish that it is all about my family and me, and we forget about everyone else. However, the Bible tells us, *"Therefore, as we have opportunity, let us do good to all people."* Galatians 6:10 (NIV). My prayer is that one day, we can look past race, class, male, or female and do good toward all humankind when the opportunity presents itself. God made us all, and *"God has no respecter of persons: But in every nation he that feareth him, and worketh righteousness, is accepted with him."* Acts 10:34-35 (KJV).

John Wayne Schlatter tells a true story about a boy named Mark who was walking home from school when he noticed another boy who had tripped, dropping all his books and other things he was carrying. Mark helped him pick it all up and took it to the boy's home. Mark discovered the boy's name was Bill and that they had some common interests. He also found Bill was having trouble with school and had just broken up with his girlfriend.

When they arrived at Bill's home, he invited Mark in for a Coke and to watch some television. They continued to spend time with each other and eventually ended up in the same high school. Three weeks before graduation, Bill asked Mark if they could talk.

Bill reminded Mark of that day several years before when they first met. "Did you ever wonder why I was carrying so many things home that day? I cleaned out my locker because I didn't want to leave a mess for anyone else. I was going home to commit suicide, but after we spent time together talking and laughing, I realized that I would miss out on future fun events if I killed myself. When you picked up those books that day, Mark, you did a lot more; you saved my life."

Only eternity can and will tell the impact of the seemingly little seeds of kindness we sow with a good motive toward humanity. Showing kindness to that one person who everyone else has neglected could reenergize and give them hope to not give up on life.

APPLICATION

Meditate on Galatians 6:10. Look for an opportunity this week to show kindness toward someone who may be hurting.

> "No act of kindness, no matter how small, is ever wasted."
> **Aesop, The Lion and the Mouse**

STRENGTH FOR THE JOURNEY

Notes & Takeaways

In the space below, write your top three take-aways from this chapter.

DAY FIFTY-EIGHT

ENCOURAGING ONE ANOTHER

"Therefore encourage one another and build one another up, just as you are doing."

1 Thessalonians 5:11 (ESV)

In 1975, a young Christian man named Stanley Stafford became the new head coach for Sparkman High School in Toney, Alabama. Early on, we found out that he was not an ordinary coach but an extraordinary person who cared deeply about his players. He was interested in our skills and wanted to understand us as a person. He visited our community, talked with our parents, and got to know them; he was always concerned about our success off the court. There was nothing he wouldn't do for any of us. Coach Stafford loved people, and you could see it and feel it in your heart. If you were having a bad day, you could always talk to him. He was never too busy to listen, and he always followed up on the situation. Coach Stafford was always willing to lend a helping hand.

I am just one of many players who would agree that he had a significant influence on shaping us and being there for us throughout high school and beyond. What made him such a tremendous coach is that he was such a great encourager. Coach Stafford exemplified 1 Thessalonians 5:11 (ESV), *"Therefore encourage one another and build one another up, just as you are doing."* Moreover, 1 Thessalonians 5:14 tells us to both encourage and be patient with all, especially the weak, so that none faints. This is only possible with the power and application of Christian love. Coach Stafford was always encouraging and building us up. Even today, he checks in on his former players. I was very grateful for the opportunity to play for such a great coach and encourager.

DAY FIFTY-EIGHT

APPLICATION

Remember, people are so discouraged these days. This week, find three people who you can encourage and build up.

"Leave everyone you meet better than you found them. Become an encourager of potential versus a destroyer of confidence."
Robin Sharma

STRENGTH FOR THE JOURNEY

Notes & Takeaways

In the space below, write your top three take-aways from this chapter.

DAY FIFTY-NINE

GOD WILL PROVIDE

"And my God shall supply all your need according to His riches in glory by Christ Jesus."

Philippians 4:19 (NKJV)

Paul writes this letter to the Philippian Church. His relations with them seem to have been very close in all the years. Paul took this opportunity to describe his situation and state of mind to his Philippian brothers. He thanked them for their gifts and gave them specific needed instructions. The entire letter talked about joy and happiness in Christ, even while Paul was in prison and in danger of death. Paul holds on to the motto, "Don't worry but be happy." He encourages the church that God not only can supply, but God will supply all of their needs. It's a comfort to know that God will provide for us. Paul's faith gave him the strength to not worry about his current situation.

Can you imagine a millionaire giving you a blank check and telling you to go home and add up all of your bills, fill in the blank check, and sign it? You would be so excited. Why is it we don't get excited about God supplying all of our needs? When I was in seminary, I heard a professor say that Philippians 4:19 is Heaven's cashier check number that will not bounce. Then he proceeded to walk us through the verse. The bank is in the first few words, where it says, My God—The Check shall supply. The amount of the check is all of your need. The thing that makes the capital and causes the check not to bounce is where it says according to his riches. The bank address is in glory, and the signature that makes this check negotiable is where it says by Christ Jesus. All we have to do is endorse the check. We endorse it by signing it with our faith, and our signature is our surrender.

If you need peace that passes all understanding, sign the check. If you need an anchor that never lets go, sign the check. If you need a bridge that will never collapse, sign the check. If we have faith, God has the power. Whatever you need, God has it. He's got the whole world in his hand. Matthew 11:28 (NKJV) says, *"Come to Me, all you who labor and are heavy laden, and I will give you rest."* Lizz Wright sang the song, "Have you got any rivers you cannot cross? Any mountains you cannot tunnel through? God specializes in the things that seem impossible, and He can do those things that no one else can do." God promises to meet your needs.

DAY FIFTY-NINE

APPLICATION

Answer this question in a journal or notebook to reflect on today's devotional.

> Are you willing to trust God so that you have all you need to the point of eternal overflowing? This means you determine how far you want to go with God.

> *"If the Lord is your shepherd, He is sufficient for all of your needs."*
> **Tony Evans**

DAY SIXTY

OVERCOMING ADVERSITY

"But those who wait on the Lord Shall renew their strength; They shall mount up with wings like eagles, They shall run and not be weary, They shall walk and not faint."

Isaiah 40:31 (NKJV)

According to the Cambridge dictionary, adversity is a difficult or unlucky situation or event that we find ourselves in. Now and then, we run into a difficult or unfortunate situation. One of my all-time favorite college football players, Jalen Hurt, can help me illustrate this. In the 2018 National Championship game, Jalen Hurt was replaced by Tua, and Alabama went on to beat Georgia for the National Championship. Jalen found himself in a difficult or unlucky situation. He said after that National Championship game, he was in the hotel room with his parents, his brother, and his sister. Jalen said, "I am in my mom and dad's arms, crying. I look up at my dad and say, 'What are we going to do now?' My dad looked me in my eyes and told me, 'We're going to fight.'" Let me stop here for a second because you can't bounce back from adversity by giving up. No one is exempt from adversity. If you live in this world long enough, you will experience adversity. However, don't focus on the adversity, but find the strength and faith to overcome the adversity. Don't get stuck in the quagmire of self-pity and start doubting yourself to get out of what you have gotten yourself into. Whenever I am faced with adversity, I put my faith In God and believe that He will give me the strength to overcome my adversity if I don't give up on Him.

Adversity will rob you of your faith to trust God for deliverance. It will prevent you from doing what you want to do, going where you want to go, and being who you want to be. You can't see your way out of the adversity you are facing right now. You are trying to fake it until you make it. You can't talk to anyone about the adversity you are going through. So, you stay silent and keep it to yourself, doing all you can to smile, but your soul is crying out on the inside. You are trying to figure out how to get through this adversity you've been in for so long. You are stuck in a quagmire (quicksand) and can't get out on your own. You have been parked too long in this adversity. Physically, you are worn out, and your strength has been zapped. Somebody is struggling to get out from underneath the adversity draining you.

Isaiah 40:31 is for people going through some stuff,

DAY SIXTY

struggling to get out from underneath the draining adversity. Isaiah is saying if you are trying to overcome adversity and need strength to overcome it, wait on the Lord. What does it mean to wait on the Lord? It means to wait with confident expectation. Waiting means anticipation, expectation, and confidence in knowing that God will come through for you. I don't know how, but God is going to work it out. Waiting on the Lord means seeking God through prayer, meditation, and hearing and reading His Word.

Jalen Hurt said, "I've been fighting for a year, not knowing what the result would be. I've been competing, keeping faith, and waiting. And you know, God was with me yesterday." Jalen came off the bench to replace Tua in the 2018 South Eastern Conference (SEC) championship game and helped Alabama beat Georgia. A year ago, Jalen found himself in an unfortunate situation or event. Yes, Jalen bounced back from adversity, and you can, too, when you trust God.

APPLICATION

God knows when to step in to help. Trust in Him to know when our strength alone may not be enough. He will come through for us.

> *"Success is to be measured not so much by the position that one has reached in life as by the obstacles which he has overcome."*
>
> **Booker T. Washington**

ABOUT THE AUTHOR

Chaplain (Colonel-Retired) David M. Lockhart is a native of Harvest, Alabama. He holds a Bachelor of Science degree in Political Science from Athens States College, Athens, Alabama; a Master of Divinity degree from Memphis Theological Seminary, Memphis, Tennessee; A Master's in Strategic Studies from the United States Army War College, Carlisle, Pennsylvania. He is currently a student at Wesley Theological Seminary in Washington, D. C. pursuing a Doctor of Ministry in Military Chaplaincy. He was ordained in 1991 by The Cumberland Presbyterian Church in America and served as Pastor for Mount Tabor Cumberland Presbyterian Church in Jackson, TN for four years. Of the many titles David has been called over the years, David is most honored to be called a servant leader and mentor. His passion is paying forward all the knowledge and open doors afforded to him on his journey through life.

ACKNOWLEDGMENTS

There is an old African Proverb that says, *"If you want to go fast, go alone. If you want to go far, go together."* My success and accomplishments are due to the love, support, tutelage, and hard work of my family, friends, and supporters. To each of you, I say, *"Thank you. I truly would not have made it this far without you."*

CONNECT WITH THE AUTHOR

Thank you for reading, Strength For The Journey. David looks forward to connecting with you and keeping you updated on his next releases.

EMAIL lockedin333@gmail.com
INSTAGRAM lockedin333
TWITTER @lockedin3332020
LinkedIn David M. Lockhart

Other Books By The Author

The Impact of Fred Shuttlesworth on the Civil Rights Movement: Table Talk Series Volume One

Dr. Martin Luther King Jr., The Prophet of Love: Table Talk Series Volume Two